quick and easy
meals
in minutes

CONTENTS

Published by Grange Books
an imprint of Grange Books Plc
The Grange
Kingsnorth Industrial Estate
Hoo, nr Rochester
Kent ME3 9ND
www.Grangebooks.co.uk
Copyright © Trident Press International 2002

Quick & Easy Meals in Minutes

Recipe Development:
Loukie Werle, Penelope Peel, Gill O'Brien

EDITORIAL
Food Editor: Sheryle Eastwood
Assistant Food Editor: Anneka Mitchell
Home Economist: Donna Hay
Editorial Coordinator: Margaret Kelly

PHOTOGRAPHY
Warren Webb

STYLING
Wendy Berecry, Belinda Clayton

DESIGN AND PRODUCTION
Manager: Nadia Sbsia
Senior Production Editor: Rachel Blackmore
Layout: Tara Barrett
Finished Art: Chris Hatcher
Cover Design: Frank Pithers

Includes Index
ISBN 1-84013-487-9
EAN 9781840134872

This Edition 2002

Printed in China

HOW TO USE THIS BOOK AND SAVE TIME

☐ As you are planning meals use the shopping list, and pantry check with each menu to help you compile your shopping list and check your pantry shelves, refrigerator and freezer as you go. Remember if you are running low on your staples replace them before you run out.

☐ Writing a shopping list saves time and money.

☐ Making a master list and shopping once a week saves time and you don't have the bother of last-minute shopping trips.

☐ Avoid the rush hour at the supermarket.

☐ Grouping the ingredients on your shopping list in their categories, such as meats, dairy foods, canned foods and frozen foods saves backtracking in the supermarket.

☐ Get to know your supermarket and write shopping lists according to the layout of the supermaket.

☐ Tidying up as you go keeps you organised and will save time after the meal.

☐ Store frozen meals in containers that can go straight from the freezer into the microwave, to the table and then into the dishwasher.

☐ When testing these recipes wherever possible, food was purchased in the form it is used in the recipe. All ingredients and essentials were collected before cooking started. This saves time and ensures you have everything you require for the menu.

Microwave: Where microwave instructions occur in this book a microwave oven with a 650 watt output has been used. Wattage on domestic microwave ovens varies between 500 and 700 watts, and it may be necessary to vary the cooking times slightly, depending on your oven.

Canned foods: Can sizes vary between countries and manufacturers. You may find the quantities in this book are slightly different from what is available. Purchase and use the can size nearest to the suggested size in the recipe.

Timesavers

The menus in this book have been planned to help you prepare and serve a delicious family meal in less than an hour. Use these hints and tips to help you save time.

☐ Buy your meat prepared for the cooking. Ask your butcher to cut, slice or bone out cuts of meat according to the recipe to help cut preparation time.

☐ Buy larger quantities of mince and freeze in separate portions to make dishes such as lasagne, spaghetti bolognese, hamburger patties, meat loaf, meat balls and tacos.

☐ Buy grated cheese.

☐ Buy bottled minced garlic, minced ginger and minced chillies. These save having to crush, chop and mince when time is short.

☐ Transfer frozen meat and poultry to the refrigerator the night before so that it thaws for dinner the next night.

☐ Use prepared whipped cream for quick dessert decorating ideas.

☐ Prepare garlic or herb bread ahead of time, wrap in foil and freeze. When needed, reheat from frozen.

☐ A food processor is the ultimate timesaver in the kitchen.

Ingredients can be grated, shredded, chopped, blended, mixed and pureed in a fraction of the time it takes to do it by hand.

☐ When shopping, look for new and interesting convenience products such as sauces and dressings, prepared pastries and pastry cases, canned fruits and vegetables and dessert items.

☐ Keep long-life milk for use in cooking if fresh milk is low.

☐ Long-life cream is also a handy pantry item.

☐ Make extra breadcrumbs in the food processor and freeze in 125 g (4 oz) portions to be thawed and used when needed.

☐ Dried herbs can be used in place of fresh herbs; just remember 1 teaspoon of dried herbs is equal to 1 tablespoon of fresh herbs.

☐ Cooked rice and pasta freeze well and can be quickly reheated in the microwave.

☐ Keep a selection of bread in the freezer. It defrosts quickly and is a good accompaniment to a meal.

☐ Store frozen meals in containers that can go straight from the freezer into the microwave, to the table and then into the dishwasher.

PANTRY CHECKLIST

Setting aside some time each week to plan your family's meals for the week ahead will save you time when you need to put together a meal in minutes. If you draw up a master grocery list as you go, you will always have all the ingredients you need to create delicious meals for family and friends.

STAPLE ITEM
- [ ] baking powder
- [ ] bicarbonate of soda
- [ ] cereal flakes
- [ ] cocoa powder
- [ ] coconut; desiccated, shredded
- [ ] cornflour
- [ ] cream of tartar
- [ ] dry breadcrumbs
- [ ] essence; almond, vanilla
- [ ] flour; plain, self-raising, wholemeal
- [ ] gelatine
- [ ] golden syrup
- [ ] honey
- [ ] instant coffee
- [ ] ground chillies
- [ ] minced garlic
- [ ] ground ginger
- [ ] prepared stock (chicken, beef, vegetable), or stock cubes
- [ ] rolled oats
- [ ] sugar; brown, caster, granulated, icing, raw

- [ ] tomato purée
- [ ] tea
- [ ] white and red wine

PERISHABLE GOODS
- [ ] butter or margarine
- [ ] cheese; Parmesan, cheddar
- [ ] eggs
- [ ] milk
- [ ] natural yogurt

CANNED FOODS
- [ ] apricot halves
- [ ] asparagus spears
- [ ] sweetcorn
- [ ] peach halves and slices
- [ ] peeled tomatoes
- [ ] pineapple pieces
- [ ] salmon
- [ ] tuna

FROZEN FOODS
- [ ] frozen vegetables; peas, beans, sweet corn
- [ ] ice cream
- [ ] pastry; filo, prepared or ready-rolled puff and shortcrust
- [ ] selection of bread rolls, loaves and sliced bread

PASTA AND RICE
- [ ] fettuccine
- [ ] no pre-cooking required lasagne sheets
- [ ] macaroni
- [ ] rice; short and long grain white, quick cooking brown
- [ ] spaghetti; plain, wholemeal

SAUCES AND MUSTARDS
- [ ] mayonnaise
- [ ] mustard; Dijon, French, wholegrain

- [ ] prepared pasta sauce
- [ ] salad dressing
- [ ] sauces; chilli, cranberry, plum, soy, Worcestershire

HERBS AND SPICES
- [ ] black peppercorns
- [ ] cayenne pepper
- [ ] chilli powder
- [ ] cinnamon; ground, sticks
- [ ] curry powder
- [ ] dried herbs; basil, mixed herbs, oregano, sage, tarragon, thyme
- [ ] ground herbs; such as coriander, cumin, paprika, turmeric,
- [ ] ground spices; allspice, ginger, mixed spice, nutmeg
- [ ] rosemary; dried leaves, ground
- [ ] whole cloves

OILS AND VINEGARS
- [ ] oils; olive, sesame
- [ ] vinegars; white, brown, cider

DRIED FRUITS, NUTS AND SEEDS
- [ ] dried fruits; apricots, currants, raisins, sultanas
- [ ] ground almonds
- [ ] nuts, such as cashews, pecans, walnuts, chopped mixed nuts
- [ ] poppy seeds
- [ ] sunflower kernels

JAMS AND RELISHES
- [ ] jams; apricot, raspberry, strawberry
- [ ] orange marmalade
- [ ] peanut butter
- [ ] relish
- [ ] sweet fruit chutney

CAKES AND BISCUITS
- [ ] plain sweet biscuits
- [ ] variety packet cake mixes
- [ ] water crackers

Food in a flash

Don't cheat your family and friends out of mouthwatering meals just because time is short. Surprise them with these tasty combinations that are on the table in under 30 minutes.

Menu 1

STEAK WITH QUICK MUSHROOM SAUCE

Serves 4

- ☐ **4 lean fillet steaks, trimmed of all visible fat**
- ☐ **freshly ground black pepper**
- ☐ **7 g ($^1/_4$ oz) butter**
- ☐ **125 g (4 oz) button mushrooms, sliced**
- ☐ **1 onion, finely chopped**
- ☐ **1 teaspoon minced garlic**
- ☐ **3 tablespoons red wine**
- ☐ **2 tablespoons tomato purée**
- ☐ **125 mL (4 fl oz) beef stock**

1   Rub steaks with black pepper. Melt butter in a nonstick frying pan and cook steaks over a medium heat for 3-4 minutes each side or until cooked to your liking. Remove steaks from pan and set aside to keep warm.

2   Add mushrooms and onion to pan and cook for 4-5 minutes or until onion is soft. Stir in garlic, wine, tomato purée and stock and cook over a medium heat for 4-5 minutes or until liquid reduces by half. Stir frequently during cooking, scraping up sediment from base of pan.

3   Place steaks on serving plates, spoon over sauce and serve.

Serving suggestion: Accompany with creamy mashed potatoes, broccoli and baby carrots.

Dessert suggestion: Fig and Melon Salad (page 9) is a quick dessert that goes well with this main course. Make the dessert first then continue as in the menu planner.

Steak with Quick Mushroom Sauce

SHOPPING LIST

- ☐ 4 lean fillet steaks
- ☐ 125 g (4 oz) button mushrooms
- ☐ 1 onion

PANTRY CHECK

- ☐ minced garlic
- ☐ red wine
- ☐ tomato pureé
- ☐ prepared beef stock or stock cubes

MENU PLANNER

- ☐ Boil, steam or microwave potatoes until tender.
- ☐ Place steaks on to cook.
- ☐ Meanwhile, microwave or steam broccoli and carrots.
- ☐ Make mushroom sauce while steaks are warming.
- ☐ Drain and mash potatoes with butter and milk until creamy.

SHOPPING LIST

- ☐ 500 g (1 lb) chicken strips
- ☐ 2 red onions
- ☐ 155 g (5 oz) button mushrooms
- ☐ 125 g (4 oz) sliced ham
- ☐ fresh parsley
- ☐ fresh basil
- ☐ double cream
- ☐ 440 g (14 oz) canned apricot halves
- ☐ 440 g (14 oz) canned peeled tomatoes
- ☐ caster sugar
- ☐ apricot jam
- ☐ icing sugar

PANTRY CHECK

- ☐ minced garlic
- ☐ prepared chicken stock or stock cubes
- ☐ white wine
- ☐ 90 g (3 oz) sultanas

MENU PLANNER

- ☐ Complete Step 1 of dessert.
- ☐ Place egg whites in a large mixing bowl and set aside. Do not beat at this stage.
- ☐ Place rice on to cook.
- ☐ Prepare and cook Chicken and Sultana Casserole.
- ☐ Complete omelette after eating main course and serve immediately.

CHICKEN AND SULTANA CASSEROLE

Serves 4

- ☐ **60 g (2 oz) butter**
- ☐ **500 g (1 lb) chicken strips**
- ☐ **1 teaspoon minced garlic**
- ☐ **2 red onions, chopped**
- ☐ **155 g (5 oz) button mushrooms, sliced**
- ☐ **1^1/2 tablespoons plain flour**
- ☐ **125 g (4 oz) sliced ham, chopped**
- ☐ **185 mL (6 fl oz) chicken stock**
- ☐ **4 tablespoons white wine**
- ☐ **440 g (14 oz) canned peeled tomatoes, drained and chopped**
- ☐ **90 g (3 oz) sultanas**
- ☐ **1 tablespoon chopped fresh parsley**
- ☐ **1 tablespoon chopped fresh basil**

1 Melt butter in a large frying pan and cook chicken over a medium high heat for 4-5 minutes. Remove from pan using slotted spoon and set aside to keep warm.
2 Add garlic, onions and mushrooms to pan and cook for 3 minutes. Stir in flour and cook for 1 minute longer. Return chicken to pan with ham, stock, wine, tomatoes, sultanas, parsley and basil and cook until sauce thickens slightly. Serve with rice.

SOUFFLE OMELETTE WITH APRICOTS

Serves 4

- ☐ **4 eggs, separated**
- ☐ **2 tablespoons double cream**
- ☐ **1 tablespoon caster sugar**
- ☐ **15 g (^{1}/2 oz) butter**
- ☐ **3 tablespoons apricot jam, warmed**
- ☐ **440 g (14 oz) canned apricot halves, drained**
- ☐ **icing sugar**
- ☐ **double cream, whipped**

1 Place egg yolks, cream and sugar in a mixing bowl and beat until combined.
2 Beat egg whites until stiff peaks form. Fold into egg yolk mixture.
3 Melt butter in a small frying pan. Spread half the egg mixture evenly over base of pan and cook over a low heat for 1-2 minutes, then place pan under a preheated grill and cook until set. Spread half the omelette with half the jam and top with half the apricots. Fold, cut in half and ease onto a serving plate. Dust with icing sugar and serve with cream. Repeat with remaining egg mixture to make second omelette.

Menu 3

PORK STROGANOFF

Serves 4

- [ ] **375 g (12 oz) fresh fettuccine**
- [ ] **2 teaspoons olive oil**
- [ ] **1/2 teaspoon minced garlic**
- [ ] **2 teaspoons poppy seeds**
- [ ] **500 g (1 lb) pork fillet, cut into strips**
- [ ] **seasoned flour**
- [ ] **60 g (2 oz) butter**
- [ ] **2 onions, sliced**
- [ ] **3 tablespoons brandy**
- [ ] **125 mL (4 fl oz) sour cream**
- [ ] **1 tablespoon tomato purée**
- [ ] **freshly ground black pepper**

1 Cook fettuccine in boiling water in a large saucepan following packet directions. Drain and toss through olive oil, garlic and poppy seeds. Set aside to keep warm.

2 Toss pork in seasoned flour to coat, shake off any excess. Melt 15 g (1/2 oz) butter in a large frying pan and cook onions for 3-4 minutes or until soft. Remove from pan and set aside.

3 Melt remaining butter in pan and cook pork in batches over a high heat for 3-4 minutes or until browned. Return pork to pan, add onions, then stir in brandy and simmer for 2-3 minutes. Remove pan from heat, stir in sour cream, tomato purée and black pepper to taste. Serve immediately with fettuccine.

FIG AND MELON SALAD

Serves 4

- [ ] **250 g (8 oz) natural yogurt**
- [ ] **1 teaspoon lime juice**
- [ ] **2 teaspoons grated lime rind**
- [ ] **1/2 melon such as honeydew melon, peeled, seeded and sliced**
- [ ] **8 fresh, dried or glacé figs, quartered**
- [ ] **3 tablespoons honey**
- [ ] **3 tablespoons chopped walnuts**

1 Combine yogurt, lime juice and lime rind in a small bowl.

2 Arrange melon and figs on individual serving plates. Spoon yogurt mixture over fruit, drizzle with honey and sprinkle with walnuts.

Left: Chicken and Sultana Casserole, Souffle Omelette with Apricots
Below: Pork Stroganoff, Fig and Melon Salad

SHOPPING LIST
- [ ] 500 g (1 lb) pork fillet, cut into strips
- [ ] 375 g (12 oz) fresh fettuccine
- [ ] 2 onions
- [ ] 1 lime
- [ ] 1/2 melon such as honeydew melon
- [ ] 8 fresh, dried or glacé figs
- [ ] 125 mL (4 fl oz) sour cream
- [ ] 250 g (8 oz) natural yogurt

PANTRY CHECK
- [ ] olive oil
- [ ] minced garlic
- [ ] poppy seeds
- [ ] brandy
- [ ] tomato purée
- [ ] honey
- [ ] walnuts

MENU PLANNER
- [ ] Prepare and make up Fig and Melon Salad, cover and chill.
- [ ] Place fettuccine on to cook following packet instructions.
- [ ] Meanwhile, prepare and cook Pork Stroganoff.

SHOPPING LIST
- ☐ 2 onions
- ☐ 1 loaf Italian bread
- ☐ 8 slices pastrami or ham
- ☐ 4 slices Gruyère cheese
- ☐ glacé cherries
- ☐ dried dates
- ☐ 125 mL (4 fl oz) orange juice
- ☐ 375 g (12 oz) natural yogurt

PANTRY CHECK
- ☐ French mustard
- ☐ gelatine
- ☐ brown sugar
- ☐ raisins

MENU PLANNER
- ☐ Prepare and make up Fruity Yogurt Desserts.
- ☐ Prepare and cook sandwiches.

Menu 4

HOT PASTRAMI AND CHEESE SANDWICHES

Serves 4

- ☐ **15 g (¹/₂ oz) butter**
- ☐ **2 onions, sliced**
- ☐ **8 slices Italian bread buttered on one side**
- ☐ **2 teaspoons French mustard**
- ☐ **8 slices pastrami or ham**
- ☐ **4 slices Gruyère cheese**

1 Melt butter in a frying pan and cook onions for 4-5 minutes or until soft.
2 Spread unbuttered side of four slices of bread with mustard, top with pastrami, onions and cheese. Place remaining bread slices on top with buttered sides out.
3 Cook sandwiches in a frying pan for 3-4 minutes each side or until golden.
Variation: If Italian bread is unavailable any bread can be used in its place.

FRUITY YOGURT DESSERTS

Serves 4

- ☐ **3 tablespoons chopped raisins**
- ☐ **10 glacé cherries, quartered**
- ☐ **8 dried dates, pitted and chopped**
- ☐ **185 mL (6 fl oz) boiling water**
- ☐ **125 mL (4 fl oz) orange juice**
- ☐ **2 teaspoons gelatine**
- ☐ **375 g (12 oz) natural yogurt**
- ☐ **2 tablespoons brown sugar**

1 Place raisins, cherries and dates in a bowl, pour over water and set aside to stand for 10 minutes, then drain.
2 Place orange juice in a microwave-safe jug, then sprinkle over gelatine and cook on HIGH (100%) for 40 seconds or place in a saucepan and cook over a medium heat, stirring constantly, until gelatine dissolves. Set aside to cool.
3 Combine yogurt and sugar, then stir in fruit and gelatine mixture. Spoon into individual serving glasses and refrigerate.

Menu 5

SPAGHETTI WITH TUNA AND OLIVES

Serves 4

- ☐ **500 g (1 lb) spaghetti**

TUNA SAUCE
- ☐ **440 g (14 oz) canned tuna in oil, drained and oil reserved**
- ☐ **1 large onion, chopped**
- ☐ **1 green pepper, sliced**
- ☐ **1 teaspoon minced garlic**
- ☐ **375 g (12 oz) tomato purée**
- ☐ **125 mL (4 fl oz) white wine**
- ☐ **1 tablespoon ground black pepper**
- ☐ **2 tablespoons finely chopped fresh parsley**
- ☐ **8 pitted black olives, halved**

1 Cook spaghetti in boiling water in a large saucepan following packet directions. Drain and set aside to keep warm.
2 To make sauce, heat reserved oil from tuna in a frying pan and cook onion, pepper and garlic for 3-4 minutes or until onion is soft. Stir in tomato purée, and wine and cook for 3-4 minutes.
3 Add tuna to sauce and cook, stirring gently, for 4-5 minutes. Spoon sauce over spaghetti and toss to combine. Garnish with black pepper, parsley and olives.

SHOPPING LIST
- ☐ 500 g (1 lb) spaghetti
- ☐ 1 large onion
- ☐ 1 green pepper
- ☐ fresh parsley
- ☐ 375 g (12 oz) tomato purée
- ☐ 8 pitted black olives
- ☐ 440 g (2 oz) canned tuna in oil

PANTRY CHECK
- ☐ minced garlic
- ☐ white wine

MENU PLANNER
- ☐ Prepare salad vegetables of your choice.
- ☐ Place spaghetti on to cook.
- ☐ Meanwhile, prepare and cook Tuna Sauce.

Left: Hot Pastrami and Cheese Sandwiches, Fruity Yogurt Desserts
Right: Spaghetti with Tuna and Olives

Microwave timesavers

Make the most of your microwave by using it for those things that it is really good at. This selection of recipes will save you time and dishes.

VEGETABLE VOL-AU-VENTS

Serves 4

- [ ] **1 courgette, sliced**
- [ ] **1/2 red pepper, diced**
- [ ] **1/2 green pepper, diced**
- [ ] **125 g (4 oz) broccoli, broken into small florets**
- [ ] **4 x 100 mm (4 in) cooked vol-au-vent pastry cases**

CHEESE SAUCE
- [ ] **30 g (1 oz) butter**
- [ ] **2 tablespoons flour**
- [ ] **freshly ground black pepper**
- [ ] **1/4 teaspoon dry mustard powder**
- [ ] **250 mL (8 fl oz) milk**
- [ ] **1 tablespoon finely chopped fresh parsley**
- [ ] **1 tablespoon snipped fresh chives**
- [ ] **60 g (2 oz) grated Cheddar cheese**

1 Place courgette, red and green pepper and broccoli in a microwave-safe dish, cover and cook on HIGH (100%) until just tender.
2 To make sauce, place butter in a microwave-safe jug and cook on HIGH (100%) for 20 seconds or until butter melts. Stir in flour, black pepper to taste and mustard. Blend in milk and cook on HIGH (100%) for 2-3 minutes or until sauce thickens. Stir twice during cooking. Stir in parsley, chives, cheese and cooked vegetables.
3 Heat vol-au-vent cases on HIGH (100%) for 1-2 minutes, then fill with vegetable mixture.

ASPARAGUS WITH HOLLANDAISE SAUCE

Serves 4

- [ ] **500 g (1 lb) asparagus, trimmed**

HOLLANDAISE SAUCE
- [ ] **125 g (4 oz) butter**
- [ ] **3 egg yolks**
- [ ] **2 tablespoons lemon juice**
- [ ] **freshly ground black pepper**

1 Place asparagus in a microwave-safe dish, cover with plastic food wrap and cook on HIGH (100%) for 5 minutes.
2 To make sauce, place butter in a microwave-safe jug and melt on MEDIUM-HIGH (70%) for 45 seconds –1 minute or until melted. Place egg yolks and lemon juice in a small bowl and whisk to combine. Whisk egg mixture into melted butter and cook on MEDIUM (50%) for 1 1/2 minutes or until sauce thickens, stirring every 30 seconds. Spoon sauce over asparagus.
Cook's tip: Hollandaise Sauce must be stirred during cooking to prevent it from curdling.

From left: Vegetable Vol-Au-Vents, Asparagus with Hollandaise Sauce, Mushroom Scramble, Prawn and Vegetable P...

MUSHROOM SCRAMBLE

Serves 4

- [ ] **4 large flat mushrooms, stems removed**
- [ ] **15 g ($^1/_2$ oz) butter**

SCRAMBLED FILLING
- [ ] **2 rashers bacon, chopped**
- [ ] **4 eggs, lightly beaten**
- [ ] **15 g ($^1/_2$ oz) butter**
- [ ] **4 tablespoons milk**
- [ ] **1 tablespoon snipped fresh chives**
- [ ] **1 tablespoon finely chopped fresh parsley**
- [ ] **freshly ground black pepper**

1   To make filling, place bacon in a microwave-safe dish and cook on HIGH (100%) for 1 minute. Add eggs, butter, milk, chives, parsley and black pepper to taste and mix to combine. Cook on HIGH (100%) for 3-4 minutes, stirring with a fork every minute.

2   Place mushrooms gill side up in a microwave-safe dish, cover and cook on HIGH (100%) for 2 minutes. Spoon filling into mushrooms and serve with toast.

PRAWN AND VEGETABLE PILAU

Serves 4

- [ ] **2 teaspoons olive oil**
- [ ] **1 onion, chopped**
- [ ] **$^1/_2$ teaspoons minced garlic**
- [ ] **$^1/_2$ red pepper, diced**
- [ ] **1 stalk celery, diced**
- [ ] **220 g (7 oz) white rice**
- [ ] **100 g ($3^1/_2$ oz) quick-cooking brown rice**
- [ ] **750 mL ($1^1/_4$ pt) chicken stock**
- [ ] **pinch turmeric**
- [ ] **200 g ($6^1/_2$ oz) canned prawns, drained**
- [ ] **1 tablespoon finely chopped fresh parsley**
- [ ] **1 tablespoon snipped fresh chives**
- [ ] **1 tablespoon finely chopped fresh basil**
- [ ] **freshly ground black pepper**

1   Place oil, onion, garlic, red pepper and celery in a large microwave-safe dish and cook on HIGH (100%) for 2 minutes. Add white and brown rice, stock and turmeric. Cook, uncovered, on HIGH (100%) for 15 minutes or until liquid is absorbed.

2   Fluff up with a fork, add prawns, cover and cook for 1 minute longer. Stir in parsley, chives and basil, and season to taste with black pepper.

ORANGE PORK CHOPS

Serves 4

☐ **2 teaspoons ground coriander**
☐ **freshly ground black pepper**
☐ **4 pork chops**
☐ **1 tablespoon oil**
☐ **15 g ($^1/_2$ oz) butter**
☐ **250 mL (8 fl oz) orange juice**
☐ **2 tablespoons orange marmalade**

1   Combine coriander and black pepper and sprinkle over chops. Heat oil and butter in a frying pan and cook chops over a high heat for 2-3 minutes each side.
2   Add orange juice and marmalade and cook for 10-15 minutes longer, or until chops are cooked through and sauce thickens slightly.

FETTUCCINE CARBONARA

Serves 4

☐ **500 g (1 lb) fettuccine**
☐ **1 tablespoon olive oil**

CARBONARA SAUCE
☐ **4 eggs**
☐ **3 tablespoons double cream**
☐ **3 tablespoons grated Parmesan cheese**
☐ **freshly ground black pepper**
☐ **4 rashers bacon, chopped**

1   Cook fettuccine in boiling water in a large saucepan following packet directions. Drain, then toss through 2 teaspoons oil and set aside to keep warm.
2   To make sauce, place eggs, cream and Parmesan cheese in a mixing bowl and beat well to combine. Season to taste with black pepper.
3   Heat remaining oil in a large frying pan and cook bacon for 4-5 minutes or until crisp. Add fettuccine and toss well. Pour egg mixture into pan and toss over a low heat for 1 minute or until egg is almost cooked. Remove from heat and serve immediately.
Serving suggestion: Accompany with green salad made from salad vegetables of your choice.

PEACHES IN CINNAMON SYRUP

Serves 4

☐ **4 tablespoons orange juice concentrate**
☐ **2 tablespoons caster sugar**
☐ **1 tablespoon lemon juice**
☐ **1 tablespoon Cointreau (orange liqueur)**
☐ **3 tablespoons water**
☐ **6 whole cloves**
☐ **1 cinnamon stick**
☐ **8 canned peach halves, drained**

1   Place orange juice concentrate, caster sugar, lemon juice, Cointreau, water, cloves and cinnamon stick in a saucepan and bring to the boil. Reduce heat and simmer, stirring occasionally, for 5 minutes or until mixture becomes syrupy.
2   Place 2 peach halves on four serving plates and pour syrup over.

Left: Orange Pork Chops
Right: Fettuccine Carbonara, Peaches in Cinnamon Syrup

SHOPPING LIST
- ☐ 300 mL (9¹/₂ fl oz) double cream
- ☐ 4 rashers bacon
- ☐ orange juice concentrate
- ☐ 1 lemon
- ☐ 440 g (14 oz) canned peach halves

PANTRY CHECK
- ☐ 500 g (1 lb) fettuccine
- ☐ olive oil
- ☐ Parmesan cheese
- ☐ caster sugar
- ☐ Cointreau (orange liqueur)
- ☐ whole cloves
- ☐ cinnamon stick

MENU PLANNER
- ☐ Place pasta on to cook.
- ☐ Prepare and cook Peaches in Cinnamon Syrup.
- ☐ Meanwhile, toss a salad of vegetables of your choice.
- ☐ Prepare and cook Carbonara Sauce.

Menu 8

BEEF AND VEGETABLES IN BLACK BEAN SAUCE

Serves 4

- ☐ **1 tablespoon vegetable oil**
- ☐ **1 teaspoon minced garlic**
- ☐ **1 teaspoon ground ginger**
- ☐ **1 onion, finely sliced**
- ☐ **375 g (12 oz) lean rump steak, cut into strips**
- ☐ **2 teaspoons sesame oil**
- ☐ **$^1/_2$ red pepper, sliced**
- ☐ **100 g ($3^1/_2$ oz) bean sprouts**
- ☐ **60 g (2 oz) mangetout**
- ☐ **$1^1/_2$ tablespoons black bean sauce**
- ☐ **1 tablespoon soy sauce**
- ☐ **3 tablespoons beef stock**
- ☐ **1 teaspoon sugar**
- ☐ **1 teaspoon cornflour blended with 1 tablespoon water**

1   Heat vegetable oil in a wok or frying pan and cook garlic and ginger over a medium heat for 1 minute. Add onion and beef and stir-fry for 3 minutes or until beef is browned. Remove from pan and set aside.

2   Heat sesame oil in pan, add red pepper, bean sprouts and mangetout and stir-fry for 1 minute. Add black beans, soy sauce, stock, sugar and cornflour mixture and cook, stirring, until mixture thickens slightly. Return beef and onions to the pan and cook for 2-3 minutes or until heated through.
Serving suggestion: Accompany with rice.

APPLE AND FIG SALAD

Serves 4

- ☐ **250 g (8 oz) dried figs**
- ☐ **4 apples, peeled and thickly sliced**
- ☐ **1 lime, thinly sliced**
- ☐ **4 tablespoons lime juice**
- ☐ **2 tablespoons caster sugar**
- ☐ **2 tablespoons brown sugar**

1   Combine figs, apples, lime, lime juice, caster sugar and brown sugar in a microwave-safe dish. Cook on HIGH (100%) for 5-7 minutes, stirring once during cooking, or place in a saucepan and cook over a medium heat for 12-15 minutes or until fruit is tender.

Beef and Vegetables in Black Bean Sauce, Apple and Fig Salad

SHOPPING LIST
- ☐ 375 g (12 oz) lean rump steak, cut into strips
- ☐ 1 onion
- ☐ 1 red pepper
- ☐ 100 g ($3^1/_2$ oz) bean sprouts
- ☐ 60 g (2 oz) mangetout
- ☐ 2 limes
- ☐ 4 apples
- ☐ black bean sauce
- ☐ 250 g (8 oz) dried figs

PANTRY CHECK
- ☐ sesame oil
- ☐ minced garlic
- ☐ ground ginger
- ☐ soy sauce
- ☐ prepared beef stock or stock cubes
- ☐ cornflour
- ☐ caster sugar
- ☐ brown sugar

MENU PLANNER
- ☐ Prepare and cook Apple and Fig Salad.
- ☐ Meanwhile, cook rice following packet directions to accompany main meal.
- ☐ Prepare and cook Beef and Vegetables in Black Bean Sauce.

Menu 9

ITALIAN SUBS

Serves 4
Oven temperature 180°C, 350°F, Gas 4

- [ ] **1 teaspoon minced garlic**
- [ ] **60 g (2 oz) butter, softened**
- [ ] **4 long bread rolls, cut in half lengthwise**
- [ ] **¼ teaspoon dried oregano**
- [ ] **250 g (8 oz) grated mozzarella cheese**
- [ ] **2 tomatoes, sliced**
- [ ] **200 g (6½ oz) sliced salami**
- [ ] **200 g (6½ oz) cooked sliced turkey, cut into strips**
- [ ] **1 red onion, finely sliced**
- [ ] **½ small green pepper, finely chopped**
- [ ] **1 tablespoon chopped fresh basil**
- [ ] **freshly ground black pepper**

1 Combine garlic and butter and spread each roll half with mixture. Sprinkle with oregano and half the cheese.

2 Top with tomato slices, salami, turkey, onion, green pepper and the remaining cheese. Place on an oven tray and bake for 15 minutes or until cheese melts. Sprinkle with basil and black pepper to taste.

Serving suggestion: Accompany with salad of your choice.

Italian Subs

Menu 10

CHOPS WITH MUSHROOM SAUCE

Serves 4

- [ ] **45 g (1¹/2 oz) butter**
- [ ] **8 thick veal or pork chops**
- [ ] **¹/2 teaspoon minced garlic**
- [ ] **375 g (12 oz) button mushrooms, sliced**
- [ ] **10 spring onions, chopped**
- [ ] **185 mL (6 fl oz) white wine**
- [ ] **1 tablespoon caster sugar**
- [ ] **1 tablespoon chopped fresh parsley**
- [ ] **freshly ground black pepper**

1 Melt butter in a large frying pan and cook chops over a medium heat for 3-4 minutes each side or until tender and golden. Remove from pan and set aside to keep warm.

2 Add garlic, mushrooms and spring onions to pan and cook for 1 minute. Stir in wine and sugar, bring to the boil, then reduce heat and simmer until reduced by half. Stir in parsley and black pepper to taste. Spoon sauce over chops and serve immediately.

Serving suggestion: Accompany with buttered noodles, carrots and courgettes.

Cook's tip: When preparing mushrooms, do not peel as the skin contains much of the flavour and nutrients. It also helps the mushrooms to retain their shape during cooking and reduces the darkening of the dish. Just wipe mushrooms with a clean, damp cloth. Store mushrooms in a paper bag or cardboard box in the refrigerator. Do not store in plastic bags as this causes them to sweat.

SHOPPING LIST

- [ ] 8 thick veal or pork chops
- [ ] 375 g (12 oz) button mushrooms
- [ ] 10 spring onions
- [ ] fresh parsley

PANTRY CHECK

- [ ] minced garlic
- [ ] white wine
- [ ] caster sugar

MENU PLANNER

- [ ] Prepare and cook chops with Mushroom Sauce.
- [ ] Meanwhile, place noodles on to cook.
- [ ] Prepare and cook vegetables of your choice.

SHOPPING LIST

☐ 4 white fish cutlets
☐ 2 lemons
☐ 1 lime
☐ sour cream
☐ fresh dill
☐ 125 mL (4 fl oz) prepared custard
☐ 125 mL (4 fl oz) double cream
☐ 440 g (14 oz) canned strawberries
☐ 2 x 440 g (14 oz) canned peach halves
☐ 375 mL (12 fl oz) sweet white wine

PANTRY CHECK

☐ minced garlic
☐ mayonnaise

MENU PLANNER

☐ Prepare and make Peaches in Almond Custard, cover and chill.
☐ Make up Dill Mayonnaise, cover and chill.
☐ Prepare and cook vegetables of your choice.
☐ Prepare and cook fish.

Menu 11

FISH WITH LEMON DILL MAYONNAISE

Serves 4

☐ **2 tablespoons oil**
☐ **2 teaspoons grated lemon rind**
☐ **2 tablespoons lemon juice**
☐ **$^1/_2$ teaspoon minced garlic**
☐ **2 tablespoons white wine**
☐ **freshly ground black pepper**
☐ **4 white fish cutlets**
☐ **60 g (2 oz) butter**

DILL MAYONNAISE

☐ **1 tablespoon lemon juice**
☐ **1 tablespoon grated lime rind**
☐ **125 g (4 oz) mayonnaise**
☐ **3 tablespoons sour cream**
☐ **1 tablespoon chopped fresh dill**

1   Place oil, lemon rind, lemon juice, garlic, wine and black pepper to taste in a small bowl and mix to combine. Brush

cutlets with lemon mixture.
2   Melt butter in a large frying pan and cook cutlets over a medium heat for 2-3 minutes each side or until fish flakes when tested with a fork. Baste regularly with remaining lemon mixture during cooking.
3   To make mayonnaise, combine lemon juice, lime rind, mayonnaise, sour cream and dill in a small bowl and mix well. Spoon mayonnaise over cutlets and serve immediately.
Serving suggestion: Accompany with crusty bread rolls, carrots, and broccoli.

PEACHES IN ALMOND CUSTARD

Serves 4

☐ **375 mL (12 fl oz) sweet white wine**
☐ **125 g (4 oz) sugar**
☐ **3 tablespoons lemon juice**
☐ **2 x 440 g (14 oz) canned peach halves, drained**

VANILLA CUSTARD
☐ **125 mL (4 fl oz) double cream**
☐ **125 mL (4 fl oz) prepared custard**

STRAWBERRY SAUCE
☐ **440 g (14 oz) canned strawberries, drained**

1   Place wine, sugar and lemon juice in a medium saucepan and bring to the boil. Add peach halves, remove from heat.
2   To make custard, place cream and custard in a bowl and mix to combine.
3   To make sauce, place strawberries in a food processor or blender and process. Push through a sieve to remove seeds.
4   Spoon a little custard onto four serving plates. Fan peach halves and place on custard. Spoon droplets of Strawberry Sauce on custard, then pull a skewer through the centre of each droplet.

*Left: Chops with Mushroom Sauce
Below: Fish with Lemon Dill Mayonnaise, Peaches in Almond Custard*

Menu 12

STIR-FRY PORK AND LETTUCE

Serves 4

- ☐ **2 tablespoons sherry**
- ☐ **1 tablespoon soy sauce**
- ☐ **2 tablespoons honey**
- ☐ **$^1/_2$ teaspoon minced garlic**
- ☐ **1 tablespoon cornflour combined with 3 tablespoons water**
- ☐ **500 g (1 lb) pork fillet, cut into thin strips**
- ☐ **2 tablespoons oil**
- ☐ **125 mL (4 fl oz) water**
- ☐ **1 curly endive, shredded**
- ☐ **3 tablespoons pine nuts, toasted**

1   Place sherry, soy sauce, honey, garlic and cornflour mixture in a small bowl and mix well. Add pork, toss to coat and set aside.

2   Heat oil in a frying pan and stir-fry pork with marinade for 4-5 minutes or until cooked. Using a slotted spoon transfer pork to a plate and keep warm.

3   Add water to pan, bring to the boil and cook, scraping up any sediment, until liquid reduces by half and sauce thickens slightly. Divide endive between serving plates, top with pork and spoon over sauce, then sprinkle with pine nuts and serve immediately.

Serving suggestion: Accompany with rice or noodles.

FRUIT COMPOTE

Serves 4

- ☐ **375 g (12 oz) assorted dried fruit, such as peaches, figs, apples, pears, prunes**
- ☐ **250 mL (8 fl oz) water**
- ☐ **1 teaspoon ground cinnamon**
- ☐ **1 teaspoon grated lemon rind**
- ☐ **2 tablespoons caster sugar**
- ☐ **2 tablespoons brandy**

Place dried fruit, water, cinnamon, lemon rind, sugar and brandy in a microwave-safe bowl and cook on HIGH (100%) for 3-5 minutes, or until fruit is tender, stir once during cooking or simmer in saucepan over a low heat for 20 minutes.

Serving suggestion: Serve hot or cold, with cream or ice cream.

SHOPPING LIST

- ☐ 500 g (1 lb) pork fillet, cut into thin strips
- ☐ 1 curly endive
- ☐ 1 lemon
- ☐ pine nuts
- ☐ 375 g (12 oz) assorted dried fruit
- ☐ ground cinnamon
- ☐ caster sugar
- ☐ brandy

PANTRY CHECK

- ☐ sherry
- ☐ soy sauce
- ☐ honey
- ☐ minced garlic
- ☐ cornflour

MENU PLANNER

- ☐ Complete step 1 of Stir-Fry Pork and Lettuce, then set aside.
- ☐ Prepare and make Fruit Compote.
- ☐ Cook noodles or rice, following packet directions, to accompany main meal.
- ☐ Complete cooking Stir-Fry Pork and Lettuce.

SPICY THAI CHICKEN

SHOPPING LIST
- ☐ 500 g (1 lb) chicken mince
- ☐ curry paste
- ☐ spring onions
- ☐ fresh basil

PANTRY CHECK
- ☐ minced garlic
- ☐ ground chillies
- ☐ 440 g (4 fl oz) canned peeled tomatoes

MENU PLANNER
- ☐ Place rice or noodles on to cook, following packet directions.
- ☐ Meanwhile, prepare and cook Spicy Thai Chicken.
- ☐ Prepare salad vegetables of your choice.

Serves 4

- ☐ **2 tablespoons oil**
- ☐ **1-2 teaspoons curry paste**
- ☐ **2 teaspoons minced garlic**
- ☐ **2 teaspoons minced chillies**
- ☐ **6 spring onions, chopped**
- ☐ **500 g (1 lb) chicken mince**
- ☐ **440 g (14 oz) canned peeled tomatoes, undrained and mashed**
- ☐ **3 tablespoons chopped fresh basil**

Heat oil in a large frying pan and stir-fry curry paste, garlic, chillies and spring onions for 2 minutes. Add chicken mince and stir-fry for 3-4 minutes or until brown. Stir in tomatoes and basil, bring to the boil, then reduce heat and simmer uncovered for 8-10 minutes or until most of the liquid has evaporated.

Serving suggestion: Accompany with boiled rice or noodles and a green salad.

Below: Spicy Thai Chicken
Left: Stir-Fry Pork and Lettuce, Fruit Compote

Microwave essentials

The microwave is great for all those little jobs that are time consuming when done conventionally. Use these hints and tips to make the most of your microwave and to save time when preparing meals.

Jam or honey: Melt for use in cooking. Remove lid from jar. Place jar in microwave and cook on HIGH (100%) for 20-30 seconds or until melted. The jam or honey can now be easily measured.

Ice cream: To soften hard ice cream for serving, place ice cream container in microwave and cook on MEDIUM (50%) for 1 minute. Remove from microwave and allow to stand for a few minutes before removing scoops.

Butter or cream cheese: To soften butter or cream cheese, cook on DEFROST (30%) for 40-60 seconds.

Pastry Cream and Hollandaise Sauce: Egg-based sauces are easy to make in the microwave. Cook on MEDIUM (50%), stirring frequently during cooking until sauce thickens slightly. Remove sauce when cooking is almost complete. The sauce will finish cooking if you allow it to stand.

Stale bread: Freshen stale bread by wrapping in absorbent kitchen paper and cooking on HIGH (100%) for 20-30 seconds.

Even cooking: Arrange food so that the thicker portions are on the outside of turntable and thinner portions towards the centre. You will find that the food will cook more evenly.

Covering: To cover or not to cover. Generally, food that requires covering for conventional cooking will also need to be covered for microwave cooking. Most food requires covering when reheating.

Defrosting: Pack meat or chicken cuts in single layers to freeze. Thaw in the microwave on DEFROST (30%). Remove thawed cuts, then continue to defrost until remaining cuts are thawed.

Instant hot dog: Make three slashes across frankfurt and place in a buttered roll. Wrap roll in absorbent kitchen paper and cook on HIGH (100%) for 30 seconds.

Plump up dried fruits: When cooking cakes and puddings use the microwave to plump up the fruit. For 500 g (1 lb) dried fruit, place fruit in a microwave-safe dish, add 250 mL (8 fl oz) water, cover and cook on HIGH (100%) for 3-4 minutes, or until fruit is no longer dried. Stir and set aside to stand for 30 minutes or until cool enough to complete recipe.

Melting chocolate: Break chocolate into small pieces and place in a microwave-safe jug. Cook on HIGH (100%) for 1-2 minutes per 200 g (6$^{1}/_{2}$ oz) of chocolate. Stir frequently during cooking.

Plastic containers and plastic food wrap: Only use containers and plastic food wraps marked microwave safe.

Peeling tomatoes: Score skin of tomatoes with a sharp knife, then cook on HIGH (100%) for 10-15 seconds per tomato.

Microwaved vegetables: Vegetables cooked in the microwave retain more of their colour and nutrients, because of the quicker cooking time and small quantity of water used.

Stale potato chips: Revive these by placing on absorbent kitchen paper and cooking on HIGH (100%) for 30 seconds, set aside and allow to cool.

Speedy roast dinner: To shorten the cooking time of a roast dinner but still achieve a crispy result, start the cooking in the microwave, then transfer to the oven to complete. For a 1.5 kg chicken, cook in the microwave on HIGH (100%) for 15 minutes, then bake in oven at 220°C (425°F, Gas 7) for 30 minutes or until golden. For 8 potatoes, cook in the microwave on HIGH (100%) for 6 minutes, then bake in oven at 220°C (425°F, Gas 7) for 20-30 minutes or until tender and crisp.

Juicier fruit: Get more juice from your fruit by warming on HIGH (100%) for 30 seconds per piece of fruit. Set aside to stand for 5 minutes then squeeze.

Standing time: Larger portions of food, such as whole chickens or roasts require standing time after cooking time is completed. For best results, cover with aluminium foil and stand for 10-15 minutes before slicing. This allows the juices to settle and the heat to equalise.

Quicker cooking: Food that is at room temperature will cook faster than refrigerated foods. Lighter foods cook more rapidly than dense food; for example, potatoes and pumpkin will take longer to cook than broccoli or eggs.

Aluminium foil: Uneven portions of meat will overcook on the thinner area. This can be prevented by shielding these areas with small strips of foil. Covering the corners of square or oblong dishes with foil will prevent these areas overcooking.

Toasting of coconut and nuts: This can be achieved quickly and efficiently in the microwave. For coconut, spread it over a microwave-safe dish and cook on HIGH (100%) for 5-6 minutes, stirring frequently during cooking until golden. Remember coconut can still burn in the microwave if overcooked. To toast nuts, place in a single layer in a microwave-safe dish and cook on HIGH (100%) for 5-6 minutes or until golden. Stir frequently during cooking to prevent burning.

WHOLEMEAL SPAGHETTI CARBONARA

Serves 4

☐ **375 g (12 oz) wholemeal spaghetti**

CARBONARA SAUCE
☐ **3 eggs**
☐ **4 tablespoons grated Parmesan cheese**
☐ **1 tablespoon chopped fresh parsley**
☐ **1 tablespoon chopped fresh basil**
☐ **1 tablespoon olive oil**
☐ **200 g (6^1/$_2$ oz) leg ham, chopped**
☐ **1 onion, chopped**
☐ **1 teaspoon minced garlic**
☐ **4 tablespoons white wine**
☐ **125 mL (4 fl oz) double cream**

1 Cook spaghetti in boiling water in a large saucepan following packet directions. Drain and set aside to keep warm.
2 Place eggs, Parmesan cheese, parsley and basil in a mixing bowl and beat until combined, set aside.
3 Heat oil in a frying pan and cook ham, onion and garlic over a medium heat for 4-5 minutes or until onion softens. Stir in wine and cream, bring to simmering and simmer until reduced by half. Remove pan from heat, stir in egg mixture, then hot spaghetti, toss well and serve immediately.
Serving suggestion: For a complete meal, serve with crusty, wholegrain bread and a mixed salad.

GINGER AND MINT FRUIT COMPOTE

Serves 4

☐ **250 mL (8 fl oz) white wine**
☐ **125 mL (4 fl oz) water**
☐ **3 tablespoons sugar**
☐ **8 dried apricots**
☐ **8 pitted prunes**
☐ **1 teaspoon minced ginger**
☐ **440 g (14 oz) canned pineapple pieces, drained**
☐ **2 tablespoons chopped fresh mint**

1 Place wine, water and sugar in a saucepan and cook, stirring over a low heat until sugar dissolves. Bring to the boil, then reduce heat and simmer uncovered for 5 minutes.
2 Add apricots, prunes and ginger, cover and simmer for 10 minutes. Stir in pineapple pieces and mint and cook for 2-3 minutes longer or until heated through.

SHOPPING LIST
☐ 500 g (1 lb) lean rump steak, cut into strips
☐ 1 onion
☐ 1 red pepper
☐ 1 green pepper
☐ oyster sauce
☐ 60 g (2 oz) cashew nuts

PANTRY CHECK
☐ vegetable oil
☐ minced garlic
☐ cornflour
☐ prepared beef stock or stock cubes
☐ soy sauce
☐ sherry

MENU PLANNER
☐ Prepare ingredients for Beef and Cashew Stir-Fry.
☐ Place noodles on to cook.
☐ Meanwhile, cook Beef and Cashew Stir-Fry.

Above: Beef and Cashew Stir-Fry
Right: Wholemeal Spaghetti Carbonara, Ginger and Mint Fruit Compote

BEEF AND CASHEW STIR-FRY

Serves 4

☐ **2 tablespoons vegetable oil**
☐ **500 g (1 lb) lean rump steak, cut into thin strips**
☐ **1 onion, cut into eighths**
☐ **1 teaspoon minced garlic**
☐ **1 red pepper, cut into strips**
☐ **1 green pepper, cut into strips**
☐ **1 teaspoon cornflour blended with 125 mL (4 fl oz) beef stock**
☐ **1 tablespoon soy sauce**
☐ **1 tablespoon oyster sauce**
☐ **4 tablespoons sherry**
☐ **60 g (2 oz) cashew nuts**

1 Heat 1 tablespoon oil in a wok or large frying pan and stir-fry beef for 2-3 minutes. Remove from pan and set aside.
2 Heat remaining oil in wok or frying pan and stir-fry onion and garlic for 3-4 minutes, add red and green peppers and stir-fry for 3-4 minutes longer.
3 Combine cornflour mixture, soy sauce, oyster sauce and sherry, stir into pan and cook for 2-3 minutes or until mixture thickens. Return beef to pan and cook for 2-3 minutes or until heated through. Stir in cashew nuts and serve immediately.
Serving suggestion: Noodles or rice.

SHOPPING LIST

- ☐ 200 g (6¹/₂ oz) leg ham
- ☐ 1 onion
- ☐ 125 mL (4 fl oz) double cream
- ☐ fresh parsley
- ☐ fresh basil
- ☐ fresh mint
- ☐ dried apricots
- ☐ pitted prunes
- ☐ 440 g (14 oz) canned pineapple pieces

PANTRY CHECK

- ☐ 375 g (12 oz) wholemeal spaghetti
- ☐ olive oil
- ☐ minced garlic
- ☐ white wine
- ☐ Parmesan cheese
- ☐ minced ginger

MENU PLANNER

- ☐ Prepare and cook Ginger and Mint Fruit Compote. Set aside to keep warm.
- ☐ Meanwhile, prepare salad vegetables of your choice to accompany main meal.
- ☐ Cook spaghetti.
- ☐ Prepare and cook Carbonara Sauce.

Fast food in style

Conquer the what's-for-dinner question by choosing one of these speedy menus. Just perfect for hectic time-tables, these meals are full of delectable flavours that will satisfy even the most discerning diners.

Menu 16

LAYERED SPICY SMOKED FISH

Serves 4
Oven temperature 200°C, 400°F, Gas 6

- ☐ **500 g (1 lb) smoked fish fillets**
- ☐ **15 g (¹/2 oz) butter**
- ☐ **1 onion, sliced**
- ☐ **2 tablespoons curry powder**

CREAM SAUCE
- ☐ **30 g (1 oz) butter**
- ☐ **2 tablespoons plain flour**
- ☐ **250 mL (8 fl oz) milk**
- ☐ **4 tablespoons double cream**
- ☐ **2 tablespoons mayonnaise**

CHEESE TOPPING
- ☐ **90 g (3 oz) breadcrumbs, made from stale bread**
- ☐ **60 g (2 oz) grated Cheddar cheese**
- ☐ **30 g (1 oz) butter, melted**

1   Place fish fillets in a large frying pan and add just enough water to cover. Cook over a medium heat until water boils, then drain and flake fish, removing skin and bones as you go.

2   Melt butter in a clean frying pan and cook onion for 4-5 minutes or until golden. Stir in curry powder and cook for 1 minute longer, then remove from heat.

3   To make sauce, melt butter in a saucepan, stir in flour and cook over a medium heat for 1 minute. Gradually add milk and cook, stirring constantly, until sauce boils and thickens. Blend in cream and mayonnaise.

4   To make topping, place breadcrumbs and cheese in a bowl, pour in butter and

mix to combine. Arrange half the fish in an ovenproof dish, top with half the onion mixture, then pour over half the sauce. Repeat layers, finishing with a layer of sauce. Sprinkle with topping and bake for 10-15 minutes or until golden brown.
Serving suggestion: Serve Layered Spicy Smoked Fish accompanied with boiled or steamed rice and buttered green beans. Finish meal with the quick Pecan Flan (page 35).

Layered Spicy Smoked Fish, Pecan Flan (page 35)

SHOPPING LIST
- ☐ 500 g (1 lb) smoked fish fillets
- ☐ 1 onion
- ☐ 250 mL (8 fl oz) double cream
- ☐ 18 cm (7 in) prepared sweet pastry case
- ☐ 90 g (3 oz) pecan nuts

PANTRY CHECK
- ☐ curry powder
- ☐ mayonnaise
- ☐ Cheddar cheese
- ☐ brown sugar
- ☐ vanilla essence
- ☐ golden syrup
- ☐ ground mixed spice
- ☐ ground cinnamon

MENU PLANNER
- ☐ Make filling and cook dessert.
- ☐ Prepare and cook Layered Spicy Smoked Fish.
- ☐ Boil or steam rice.
- ☐ Prepare and cook vegetables of your choice.

RED CURRANT PORK CHOPS

Serves 4

- [ ] **2 tablespoons oil**
- [ ] **4 pork chops, trimmed of excess fat**
- [ ] **3 tablespoons red currant jelly**
- [ ] **200 g (6^1/$_2$ oz) canned blackcurrants, drained and 3 tablespoons of juice reserved**
- [ ] **1 teaspoon raspberry jam**
- [ ] **2 teaspoons lemon juice**
- [ ] **2 tablespoons red wine**
- [ ] **2 tablespoons red wine vinegar**
- [ ] **2 tablespoons brown sugar**

1   Heat oil in a large frying pan and cook chops over a medium high heat for 5 minutes each side or until browned and cooked through. Remove from pan and set aside to keep warm.

2   Add red currant jelly, reserved blackcurrant juice, raspberry jam, lemon juice, wine, vinegar and sugar to pan. Bring to the boil, stirring constantly, then reduce heat and simmer for 3 minutes. Stir in blackcurrants. Spoon sauce over chops and serve.

Serving suggestion: Serve with potatoes, steamed or microwaved broccoli and carrots.

MANGO FOOL

Serves 4

- [ ] **2 ripe mangoes or 440 g (14 oz) canned mango flesh, chopped**
- [ ] **2 tablespoons lemon juice**
- [ ] **250 mL (8 fl oz) double cream**
- [ ] **1 tablespoon icing sugar**
- [ ] **mango slices to garnish**

1   If using fresh mangoes peel and cut flesh into large cubes. Place mango flesh and lemon juice in a food processor or blender and process until smooth.

2   Place cream and icing sugar in a mixing bowl and beat until soft peaks form. Fold mango purée into cream. Spoon into individual serving dishes. Decorate with a slice of mango and chill.

Cook's tip: Fools can be made from any fruit, according to what is available. Try using dried apricots for a change. Place 250 g (8 oz) dried apricots, 250 mL (8 fl oz) water and 3 tablespoons sugar in a saucepan and bring to the boil, reduce heat and simmer for 10 minutes. Set aside to stand for 1 hour, drain and purée. Omit lemon juice and make as for Mango Fool.

MUSHROOM RISOTTO

Serves 4

- ☐ **125 g (4 oz) butter**
- ☐ **1 onion, chopped**
- ☐ **315 g (10 oz) short-grain rice**
- ☐ **170 mL (5^1/$_2$ oz) red wine**
- ☐ **750 mL (1^1/$_4$ pt) boiling vegetable stock**
- ☐ **500 g (1 lb) button mushrooms, sliced**
- ☐ **3 tablespoons grated Parmesan cheese**
- ☐ **2 tablespoons chopped fresh basil**
- ☐ **freshly ground black pepper**

1 Melt 90 g (3 oz) butter in a large saucepan and cook onion over a medium heat for 3-4 minutes or until soft. Add rice and stir to coat with butter. Stir in wine and cook for 2 minutes.

2 Add 500 mL (16 fl oz) boiling stock and cook over a medium heat for 5 minutes or until liquid is absorbed, stirring occasionally. Add mushrooms and remaining stock. Continue to cook until most of the stock has been absorbed.

3 Stir in remaining butter, Parmesan cheese, basil and black pepper to taste.

Serving suggestion: Accompany with crusty bread and a green salad.

Dessert suggestion: Almond Liqueur Oranges (page 37) is a quick dessert that goes well with this main course. Make the dessert while the risotto is cooking.

Left: Red Currant Pork Chops, Mango Fool
Below: Mushroom Risotto

BAKED LEEK AND HAM ROLLS

Serves 4
Oven temperature 180°C, 350°F, Gas 4

- ☐ **8 leeks, washed and trimmed to leave white stems**
- ☐ **8 slices leg ham**
- ☐ **60 g (2 oz) grated Cheddar cheese**
- ☐ **2 tablespoons breadcrumbs made from stale bread**

CHEESE SAUCE
- ☐ **45 g (1¹/₂ oz) butter**
- ☐ **2 tablespoons plain flour**
- ☐ **375 mL (12 fl oz) hot milk**
- ☐ **3 tablespoons double cream**
- ☐ **¹/₂ teaspoon ground nutmeg**
- ☐ **60 g (2 oz) grated Cheddar cheese**
- ☐ **1 tablespoon chopped fresh chives**
- ☐ **freshly ground black pepper**

1 Cook leeks in boiling water in a large saucepan for 7 minutes, then drain and set aside.

2 To make sauce, melt butter in a microwave-safe jug, stir in flour and then whisk in milk and cream. Cook on HIGH (100%) for 3-4 minutes or until sauce thickens, stir twice during cooking, or melt butter in a saucepan, stir in flour and cook over a medium heat for 1 minute. Remove from heat and slowly whisk in milk and cream. Return to heat and cook, stirring constantly, until sauce thickens. Stir in nutmeg, cheese, chives and black pepper to taste.

3 Wrap each leek in a slice of ham and place in a greased ovenproof dish. Spoon sauce over, sprinkle with cheese and breadcrumbs and bake for 10-15 minutes or until golden brown and heated through.
Serving suggestion: Accompany with crusty bread rolls and a green salad.
Cook's tip: It is important to wash leeks well before using. To wash leeks, cut off 4-5 cm (1¹/₂- 1³/₄ in) of the green part. If using leeks whole, slit down the middle to within 2.5 cm (1 in) of the root end and wash thoroughly under running water, spreading the layers gently to ensure that all dirt is washed out, then drain well. If leeks are to be chopped, slice them first, place in a colander and rinse well under cold running water, then drain.

Left: Baked Leek and Ham Rolls, Orange French Toast
Right: Sausage Frittata, Brandy Apricots

SHOPPING LIST

- ☐ 8 leeks
- ☐ 300 mL (9¹/₂ fl oz) double cream
- ☐ fresh chives
- ☐ 8 slices leg ham
- ☐ 1 orange
- ☐ 1 prepared plain or madeira loaf cake

PANTRY CHECK

- ☐ ground nutmeg
- ☐ Cheddar cheese
- ☐ vanilla essence

MENU PLANNER

- ☐ Prepare and cook Baked Leek and Ham Rolls.
- ☐ Prepare salad vegetables of your choice, cover. Chill.
- ☐ Prepare and cook Orange French Toast. Set aside and keep warm while eating main course.

Menu 19

ORANGE FRENCH TOAST

Serves 4

- ☐ **3 eggs**
- ☐ **3 tablespoons milk**
- ☐ **2 tablespoons double cream**
- ☐ **2 teaspoons vanilla essence**
- ☐ **2 tablespoons orange juice**
- ☐ **1 tablespoon grated orange rind**
- ☐ **1 plain or madeira loaf cake, cut into 1 cm (¹/₂ in) slices**
- ☐ **15 g (¹/₂ oz) butter**
- ☐ **whipped cream to serve**

1 Place eggs, milk, cream and vanilla in a mixing bowl and beat until frothy. Stir in orange juice and orange rind.

2 Dip cake slices into egg mixture. Melt butter in a large frying pan and cook cake slices over a medium heat for 2-3 minutes each side or until golden. Serve with whipped cream.

SAUSAGE FRITTATA

Serves 4

☐ **250 mL (8 fl oz) double cream**
☐ **8 eggs, lightly beaten**
☐ **freshly ground black pepper**
☐ **30 g (1 oz) butter**
☐ **2 spring onions, chopped**
☐ **2 tablespoons chopped fresh basil**
☐ **1 red pepper, finely chopped**
☐ **4 spicy sausages, grilled and cut into thin rounds**
☐ **60 g (2 oz) grated Cheddar cheese**

1 Place cream, eggs and black pepper to taste in a mixing bowl and beat until well combined. Melt butter in a 23 cm (9 in) heavy-based frying pan. Pour in egg mixture and cook over a medium heat for 3-4 minutes, lifting frittata with a spatula as it sets to allow uncooked mixture to flow underneath.

2 Sprinkle frittata with spring onions, basil and red pepper, then arrange sausage slices on top and finally sprinkle with cheese. Place under a preheated grill and cook until cheese melts and frittata is firm. Serve immediately.

Serving suggestion: Accompany with a green salad and crusty wholemeal rolls.

BRANDY APRICOTS

Serves 4

☐ **2 x 440 g (14 oz) canned apricot halves, drained and juice reserved**
☐ **1 teaspoon ground cinnamon**
☐ **2 strips orange rind**

BRANDY SYRUP
☐ **250 mL (8 fl oz) reserved juice from apricots**
☐ **1 tablespoon lemon juice**
☐ **2 tablespoons apricot jam**
☐ **2 tablespoons brandy**
☐ **2 tablespoons orange juice**

1 To make syrup, place reserved apricot juice, lemon juice, jam, brandy and orange juice in a saucepan and bring to the boil, then reduce heat and simmer for 3 minutes.

2 Add apricot halves, cinnamon and orange rind, remove from heat and set aside to cool to room temperature.

Serving suggestion: Accompany with cream or ice cream.

SPINACH ROULADE

Serves 6
Oven temperature 200°C, 400°F, Gas 6

- [ ] **250 g (8 oz) frozen spinach, thawed**
- [ ] **1 tablespoon plain flour**
- [ ] **5 eggs, separated**
- [ ] **15 g (¹/₂ oz) butter**
- [ ] **1 teaspoon ground nutmeg**
- [ ] **freshly ground black pepper**
- [ ] **2 tablespoons Parmesan cheese**

MUSHROOM FILLING
- [ ] **30 g (1 oz) butter**
- [ ] **100 g (3¹/₂ oz) button mushrooms, sliced**
- [ ] **3 spring onions, chopped**
- [ ] **440 g (14 oz) canned peeled tomatoes, drained and chopped**
- [ ] **¹/₂ teaspoon dried oregano**
- [ ] **¹/₂ teaspoon dried basil**

1   Place spinach, flour, egg yolks, butter, nutmeg and black pepper to taste in a food processor or blender and process until combined. Transfer to a bowl.
2   Beat egg whites until stiff peaks form, then mix 2 tablespoons of egg whites into spinach mixture. Fold remaining egg whites into spinach mixture.
3   Spoon into a greased and lined Swiss roll tin and cook for 12 minutes or until mixture is firm.
4   To make filling, melt butter in a frying pan and cook mushrooms over a medium heat for 1 minute. Add spring onions, tomatoes, oregano and basil and cook for 3 minutes longer.
5   Turn roulade out onto a teatowel sprinkled with Parmesan cheese and roll up. Allow to stand for 1 minute. Unroll and spread with filling. Reroll and serve immediately.

RICE CREAM WITH MAPLE SYRUP

Serves 6

- [ ] **315 g (10 oz) short-grain rice**
- [ ] **300 mL (9¹/₂ fl oz) double cream, whipped**
- [ ] **1 teaspoon ground cinnamon**
- [ ] **maple syrup**

Cook rice in boiling water in a large saucepan for 12-15 minutes or until tender, drain and rinse under cold water. Mix rice with whipped cream and cinnamon. Spoon into individual serving dishes and chill. Serve topped with maple syrup.

SHOPPING LIST

- [ ] 250 g (8 oz) frozen spinach
- [ ] 100 g (3¹/₂ oz) button mushrooms
- [ ] spring onions
- [ ] 300 mL (9¹/₂ fl oz) double cream
- [ ] maple syrup

PANTRY CHECK

- [ ] ground nutmeg
- [ ] Parmesan cheese
- [ ] 440 g (14 oz) canned peeled tomatoes

- [ ] dried oregano
- [ ] dried basil
- [ ] short-grain rice
- [ ] ground cinnamon

MENU PLANNER

- [ ] Prepare and make Rice Cream with Maple Syrup.
- [ ] Meanwhile, prepare salad. Cover and chill.
- [ ] Complete step one of roulade.
- [ ] Prepare and cook Spinach Roulade. While roulade is cooking, make the filling.

Menu 22

FETTUCCINE WITH BACON AND AVOCADO

Serves 4

- [ ] **375 g (12 oz) fettuccine**

BACON AND AVOCADO SAUCE
- [ ] **2 rashers bacon, trimmed and chopped**
- [ ] **1 red onion, sliced**
- [ ] **2 avocados, peeled, stones removed and puréed**
- [ ] **2 tablespoons cream**
- [ ] **2 tablespoons lemon juice**
- [ ] **freshly ground black pepper**
- [ ] **3 tablespoons grated Parmesan cheese**

1 Cook fettuccine in boiling water in a large saucepan following packet directions. Drain and set aside to keep warm.

2 To make sauce, place bacon and onion in a frying pan and cook over a medium heat for 3-4 minutes or until onion is soft. Add puréed avocados, cream and lemon juice, and cook, stirring, over a low heat for 3-4 minutes or until heated through. Do not allow sauce to boil.

3 Add fettuccine to sauce and toss. Serve sprinkled with black pepper and Parmesan cheese. Serve immediately.

Serving suggestion: This dish makes a nutritious and satisfying meal when served with crusty wholemeal rolls and a green salad.

Timesaver: Fresh pasta is widely available in supermarkets and gourmet food outlets. It is available in many flavours and shapes and has a flavour far superior to that of dried pasta. Fresh pasta also cooks in one-third of the time of dried pasta.

Left: Spinach Roulade, Rice Cream with Maple Syrup
Above: Fettuccine with Bacon and Avocado, Bananas with Cinnamon Triangles

BANANAS WITH CINNAMON TRIANGLES

Serves 4
Oven temperature 200°C, 400°F, Gas 6

- [ ] **100 g (3½ oz) prepared or ready-rolled puff pastry**
- [ ] **1 teaspoon ground cinnamon**
- [ ] **2 tablespoons sugar**
- [ ] **2 teaspoons water**
- [ ] **30 g (1 oz) butter**
- [ ] **3 bananas, sliced**
- [ ] **3 tablespoons chopped walnuts**
- [ ] **1 tablespoon brown sugar**
- [ ] **1 tablespoon lemon juice**

1 Cut pastry into four 10 cm (4 in) squares, then cut squares into triangles. Combine cinnamon and sugar in a small bowl. Brush pastry triangles with water and sprinkle with cinnamon mixture. Place on a greased baking tray and bake for 10 minutes or until puffed and golden.

2 Melt butter in a frying pan. Add bananas, walnuts, brown sugar and lemon juice and cook, tossing over a medium heat for 5 minutes or until bananas are tender. Serve hot topped with pastry triangles.

Short and sweet

A dessert can transform an everyday meal into something really special and with the clever use of convenience products and a little know-how it need not take hours to create a great looking dessert.

CHOCOLATE MINT GATEAU

Serves 10

- ☐ **1 prepared unfilled chocolate sponge**
- ☐ **10 chocolate-coated peppermint disks or thins**

MINT CREAM FILLING
- ☐ **375 mL (12 fl oz) double cream**
- ☐ **3¹/₂ tablespoons cocoa powder, sifted with 2 tablespoons icing sugar**
- ☐ **1 tablespoon dark rum**
- ☐ **90 g (3 oz) chocolate-coated peppermint disks or thins, chopped**

1 To make filling, place cream and cocoa powder mixture in a mixing bowl and beat until soft peaks form. Fold through rum and chopped peppermint disks or thins.
2 To assemble cake, spread one layer with a quarter of the filling, then place remaining sponge layer on top. Spread remaining filling over top and sides of cake and decorate with peppermint disks or thins.

Cook's tip: Any flavoured chocolate-coated disks or thins can be used in this cream filling. Or you might like to use your favourite chocolate confectionery instead.

PEACH TARTLETS

Serves 4

- ☐ **12 frozen individual sweet tartlet cases**
- ☐ **6 canned peach halves, drained and sliced**
- ☐ **1 tablespoon icing sugar, sifted**

FILLING
- ☐ **2 canned peach halves, drained**
- ☐ **60 g (2 oz) cream cheese**
- ☐ **1¹/₂ tablespoons caster sugar**
- ☐ **1 egg yolk**
- ☐ **1 teaspoon grated orange rind**
- ☐ **¹/₂ teaspoon vanilla essence**
- ☐ **3 tablespoons double cream, whipped**

1 Cook tart cases according to packet directions. Cool.
2 To make filling, place peach halves, cream cheese, sugar, egg yolk, orange rind and vanilla essence in a food processor or blender and process until smooth. Transfer to a bowl and fold in cream.
3 Spoon filling into pastry cases and top with sliced peaches. Dust with icing sugar just prior to serving.

Cook's tip: If prepared tartlet cases are unavailable, make your own using prepared sweet shortcrust pastry. Line twelve tartlet pans with pastry, then line with baking paper and uncooked rice or dried beans and bake at 200°C (400°F, Gas 6) for 8-10 mins. Remove rice or beans and paper and cook for 4-5 minutes longer or until golden and cooked. Allow to cool before filling.

BERRY ICE CREAM CAKE

Serves 8

- ☐ **1 prepared madeira loaf, split horizontally**
- ☐ **1¹/₂ litres (2¹/₂ pt) chocolate ice cream, softened**
- ☐ **14 sponge fingers**
- ☐ **5 tablespoons instant setting chocolate ice cream topping**
- ☐ **250 g (8 oz) mixed berries, such as strawberries, blueberries or blackberries**

Spread bottom layer of madeira loaf with half the ice cream. Place remaining loaf layer on top and spread with remaining ice cream. Spread flat side of each sponge finger with chocolate ice cream topping and position chocolate side facing inwards around outside of cake. Freeze until set. Just prior to serving, decorate with mixed berries and tie a ribbon around outside of cake. Stand 5 minutes before cutting.

PECAN FLAN

Serves 4
Oven temperature 160°C, 325°F, Gas 3

- ☐ **1 x 18 cm (7 in) prepared sweet pastry case**

PECAN FILLING
- ☐ **3 tablespoons brown sugar**
- ☐ **30 g (1 oz) butter**
- ☐ **1 teaspoon vanilla essence**
- ☐ **2 eggs**
- ☐ **4 tablespoons golden syrup**
- ☐ **1 tablespoon plain flour, sifted**
- ☐ **1 teaspoon ground mixed spice**
- ☐ **1 teaspoon ground cinnamon**
- ☐ **90 g (3 oz) pecan nuts, roughly chopped**

1   To make filling, beat sugar, butter and vanilla essence until light and fluffy. Add eggs one at a time beating well after each addition. Fold through golden syrup, flour, mixed spice, cinnamon and pecan nuts.
2   Spoon filling into pastry case and bake for 35-40 minutes or until firm.

From left: Chocolate Mint Gateau, Peach Tartlets, Berry Ice Cream Cake, Pecan Flan

SHOPPING LIST

- [ ] 4 thin pork escalopes
- [ ] 2 lemons
- [ ] 500 mL (16 fl oz) double cream
- [ ] 4 prepared meringue cases
- [ ] marshmallows
- [ ] 125 g (4 oz) dark chocolate

PANTRY CHECK

- [ ] Parmesan cheese
- [ ] dry breadcrumbs
- [ ] prepared beef stock or stock cubes
- [ ] mixed nuts
- [ ] desiccated coconut
- [ ] chocolate liqueur (optional)
- [ ] flaked almonds

MENU PLANNER

- [ ] Prepare and coat pork with breadcrumb mixture, cover and refrigerate.
- [ ] Prepare filling and sauce for meringue cases. Arrange dessert on serving plates.
- [ ] Prepare vegetables.
- [ ] Place vegetables on to cook.
- [ ] Cook pork and set aside to keep warm.
- [ ] Meanwhile, make Lemon Cream Sauce.

LEMON PORK ESCALOPES

Serves 4

- [ ] **75 g (2¹/₂ oz) grated Parmesan cheese**
- [ ] **4 tablespoons dry breadcrumbs**
- [ ] **1 tablespoon grated lemon rind**
- [ ] **freshly ground black pepper**
- [ ] **4 thin pork escalopes**
- [ ] **plain flour**
- [ ] **2 eggs, lightly beaten**
- [ ] **90 g (3 oz) butter**

LEMON CREAM SAUCE
- [ ] **3 tablespoons beef stock**
- [ ] **1 tablespoon lemon juice**
- [ ] **125 mL (4 fl oz) double cream**

1   Combine Parmesan cheese, breadcrumbs, lemon rind and black pepper to taste in a bowl. Dust pork with flour, dip in egg and coat with breadcrumb mixture.
2   Heat butter in a large frying pan and cook pork escalopes for 2-3 minutes each side. Remove from pan and keep warm.
3   To make sauce, add stock and lemon juice to pan, bring to the boil and boil until reduced by half. Remove pan from heat and stir in cream. Serve spooned over pork.
Serving suggestion: For a complete meal, serve with potatoes, courgettes and carrots.

NUTTY MERINGUES

Serves 4

- [ ] **4 prepared meringue cases**

MARSHMALLOW FILLING
- [ ] **3 tablespoons chopped mixed nuts**
- [ ] **8 marshmallows, quartered**
- [ ] **2 tablespoons desiccated coconut**
- [ ] **125 mL (4 fl oz) double cream, whipped**

CHOCOLATE SAUCE
- [ ] **125 g (4 oz) dark chocolate**
- [ ] **125 mL (4 fl oz) double cream**
- [ ] **1 tablespoon chocolate liqueur (optional)**
- [ ] **1 tablespoon flaked almonds, toasted**

1   To make filling, fold nuts, marshmallows and coconut into cream. Spoon mixture into meringue cases.
2   To make sauce, place chocolate, cream and liqueur into a small saucepan and cook, stirring, over a low heat for 5 minutes or until well combined. Drizzle sauce over meringues and spoon remaining sauce onto plates. Decorate with flaked almonds.

CHICKEN LIVER AND MARSALA RISOTTO

Serves 4

- ☐ **90 g (3 oz) butter**
- ☐ **1 onion, chopped**
- ☐ **1/2 teaspoon minced garlic**
- ☐ **500 g (1 lb) chicken livers, halved**
- ☐ **315 g (10 oz) short-grain rice, rinsed and drained**
- ☐ **4 tablespoons Marsala or dry sherry**
- ☐ **875 mL (1 1/2 pt) boiling chicken stock**
- ☐ **60 g (2 oz) grated Parmesan cheese**
- ☐ **2 tablespoons chopped fresh basil**
- ☐ **freshly ground black pepper**

1 Melt 60 g (2 oz) butter in a saucepan and cook onion and garlic over a medium heat until onion is soft. Add chicken livers and cook for 3-4 minutes or until brown, remove and set aside.

2 Add rice to pan and cook, tossing to coat with butter, for 1 minute. Stir in Marsala or sherry and 250 mL (8 fl oz) boiling stock. Cook over a medium heat, stirring occasionally, until liquid is absorbed. Add another 250 mL (8 fl oz) stock and continue as above until all stock has been added and absorbed.

3 Stir in remaining butter, chicken liver mixture, Parmesan cheese and basil. Season to taste with black pepper and serve immediately.

Serving suggestion: Accompany with a green salad.

ALMOND LIQUEUR ORANGES

Serves 4

- ☐ **4 oranges, peeled**
- ☐ **2 tablespoons sugar**
- ☐ **3 tablespoons Grand Marnier (orange liqueur)**
- ☐ **125 mL (4 fl oz) double cream**
- ☐ **3 tablespoons slivered almonds, toasted**

Slice oranges, then arrange on four serving plates. Sprinkle with sugar and Grand Marnier. Decorate with cream and almonds.

Left: Lemon Pork Escalopes, Nutty Meringues
Above: Chicken Liver and Marsala Risotto, Almond Liqueur Oranges

---

SHOPPING LIST

- ☐ 500 g (1 lb) chicken livers
- ☐ 1 onion
- ☐ fresh basil
- ☐ 4 oranges
- ☐ 125 mL (4 fl oz) double cream

PANTRY CHECK

- ☐ prepared chicken stock or stock cubes
- ☐ minced garlic
- ☐ short-grain rice

- ☐ Marsala or dry sherry
- ☐ Parmesan cheese
- ☐ Grand Marnier
- ☐ slivered almonds

MENU PLANNER

- ☐ Prepare and cook Chicken Liver and Marsala Risotto.
- ☐ Meanwhile, prepare salad vegetables to accompany the risotto, cover and chill.
- ☐ Prepare and make Almond Liqueur Oranges.

LEBANESE LAMB ROLLS

Serves 4
Oven temperature 180°C, 350°F, Gas 4

- [ ] **2 tablespoons oil**
- [ ] **1 onion, chopped**
- [ ] **500 g (1 lb) minced lamb**
- [ ] **1 small aubergine, cubed**
- [ ] **2 teaspoons ground allspice**
- [ ] **1 teaspoon chilli sauce**
- [ ] **3 tablespoons red wine**
- [ ] **440 g (14 oz) canned tomatoes, undrained and mashed**
- [ ] **4 tablespoons sultanas**
- [ ] **3 tablespoons pine nuts, toasted**
- [ ] **4 large pitta bread rounds**
- [ ] **4 lettuce leaves, shredded**
- [ ] **1 carrot, peeled and grated**

1 Heat oil in a large frying pan and cook onion for 3-4 minutes or until softened. Add lamb and cook over a medium high heat for 5 minutes longer or until brown. Stir in aubergine, allspice, chilli sauce, wine, tomatoes and sultanas. Bring to the boil, then reduce heat and simmer for 5 minutes or until sauce has reduced and thickened slightly. Stir in pine nuts.
2 Heat pitta breads in oven for 5 minutes or until heated through but not crisp. Spread with lamb mixture, top with lettuce and carrot, and roll up. Serve immediately.

LYCHEES IN COINTREAU

Serves 4

- [ ] **440 g (14 oz) canned lychees, drained**
- [ ] **1 orange, peeled and chopped**
- [ ] **2 tablespoons chopped glacé ginger**
- [ ] **2 tablespoons Cointreau**

Arrange lychees and orange in four individual serving bowls and sprinkle with ginger and Cointreau.

SHOPPING LIST

- [ ] 500g (1 lb) minced lamb
- [ ] 1 onion
- [ ] 1 small aubergine
- [ ] chilli sauce
- [ ] pine nuts
- [ ] 4 large pitta bread rounds
- [ ] 1 lettuce
- [ ] 1 carrot
- [ ] 1 orange
- [ ] 440 g (14 oz) canned lychees
- [ ] glace ginger

- [ ] red wine
- [ ] 440 g (14 oz) canned peeled tomatoes
- [ ] sultanas
- [ ] Cointreau

PANTRY CHECK

- [ ] ground allspice

MENU PLANNER

- [ ] Prepare and make up Lychees in Cointreau. Cover and chill.
- [ ] Prepare and cook meat sauce for Lebanese Lamb Rolls.
- [ ] Meanwhile, heat pitta bread in oven and prepare lettuce and carrot for lamb rolls.

Left: Lebanese Lamb Rolls, Lychees in Cointreau
Right: Quick Chicken Curry, Maple Syrup Cream

SHOPPING LIST

- ☐ 1 cooked chicken
- ☐ 1 onion
- ☐ 1 green pepper
- ☐ 125 mL (4 fl oz) prepared vanilla custard
- ☐ 250 mL (8 fl oz) double cream
- ☐ maple syrup
- ☐ 250 g (8 oz) natural yogurt

PANTRY CHECK

- ☐ minced garlic
- ☐ curry paste
- ☐ ground cumin
- ☐ prepared chicken stock or stock cubes
- ☐ slivered almonds
- ☐ dark rum

MENU PLANNER

- ☐ Prepare and make up Maple Syrup Cream. Cover and chill.
- ☐ Prepare side dishes, if serving, to accompany curry.
- ☐ Place rice on to cook, following packet directions.
- ☐ Meanwhile, prepare and cook Quick Chicken Curry.

Menu 26

QUICK CHICKEN CURRY

Serves 4

- ☐ **45 g (1¹/2 oz) butter**
- ☐ **1 onion, chopped**
- ☐ **¹/2 teaspoon minced garlic**
- ☐ **1 green pepper, chopped**
- ☐ **3 teaspoons curry paste**
- ☐ **1 teaspoon ground cumin**
- ☐ **2 tablespoons plain flour**
- ☐ **500 mL (16 fl oz) chicken stock**
- ☐ **1 cooked chicken, flesh removed and cut into bite-size pieces**

1 Melt butter in a large frying pan and cook onion, garlic and green pepper over a medium heat for 3-4 minutes or until onion is soft.

2 Add curry paste, cumin and flour and cook for 1 minute longer. Stir in stock and cook, stirring constantly, until mixture boils and thickens. Add chicken, and simmer for 3 minutes or until chicken is heated through.

Serving suggestion: Accompany with boiled rice. You might also like to serve side dishes of chopped tomato and onion, chopped peanuts, bananas and coconut, cucumber in yogurt, and poppadums.

MAPLE SYRUP CREAM

Serves 4

- ☐ **250 mL (8 fl oz) double cream**
- ☐ **125 mL (4 fl oz) prepared vanilla custard**
- ☐ **250 g (8 oz) natural yogurt**
- ☐ **3 tablespoons maple syrup**
- ☐ **2 tablespoons dark rum**
- ☐ **3 tablespoons slivered almonds, toasted**

Beat cream until soft peaks form. Fold custard, yogurt, maple syrup and rum into cream. Spoon into individual serving dishes, decorate with almonds, cover and refrigerate.

SHOPPING LIST

☐ 1 cooked chicken
☐ 375 g (12 oz) mushrooms
☐ 440 g (14 oz) canned tomato purée
☐ sunflower seeds
☐ 2 x 440 g (14 oz) canned stoned plums

☐ rolled oats
☐ brown sugar
☐ ground cinnamon

PANTRY CHECK

☐ white wine
☐ prepared chicken stock or stock cubes
☐ dried mixed herbs
☐ tomato paste

MENU PLANNER

☐ Prepare and cook Crunchy Plum Bake.
☐ Meanwhile, prepare and cook Tuscan Chicken.
☐ While chicken is cooking, cook noodles following packet directions.
☐ Prepare salad vegetables of your choice as an accompaniment.

TUSCAN CHICKEN

Serves 6

☐ **1 cooked chicken, broken into pieces**

TOMATO WINE SAUCE
☐ **125 mL (4 fl oz) white wine**
☐ **250 mL (8 fl oz) chicken stock**
☐ **440 g (14 oz) canned tomato purée**
☐ **375 g (12 oz) mushrooms, quartered**
☐ **1 teaspoon dried mixed herbs**
☐ **2 tablespoons tomato paste**

1 To make sauce, place wine, stock and tomato purée in a large saucepan, bring to the boil and cook for 10 minutes or until mixture thickens slightly.
2 Add mushrooms, mixed herbs and tomato paste and cook for 5 minutes longer. Add chicken and mix gently to coat with sauce, cook for 10 minutes or until heated through.
Serving suggestion: Accompany with buttered noodles and a green salad of two or three kinds of lettuce, cucumber and red onion.

CRUNCHY PLUM BAKE

Serves 6
Oven temperature 180°C, 350°F, Gas 4

☐ **2 x 440 g (14 oz) canned stoned plums, drained**

CRUMBLE TOPPING
☐ **90 g (3 oz) rolled oats**
☐ **75 g (2¹/₂ oz) sunflower seeds**
☐ **1 tablespoon plain flour**
☐ **3 tablespoons brown sugar**
☐ **1 teaspoon ground cinnamon**
☐ **60 g (2 oz) butter, chilled and chopped**

1 To make topping, place oats, sunflower seeds, flour, sugar, cinnamon and butter in a food processor or blender and process until mixture resembles fine breadcrumbs.
2 Arrange plums in a lightly greased 20 cm (8 in) round dish. Sprinkle with topping and bake for 15 minutes or until golden brown.

Left: Tuscan Chicken, Crunchy Plum Bake
Right: Lamb Noisettes with Mustard and Rosemary, Custard Tart

LAMB NOISETTES WITH MUSTARD AND ROSEMARY

Serves 4

- ☐ **4 tablespoons wholegrain mustard**
- ☐ **2 tablespoons finely chopped fresh rosemary leaves**
- ☐ **$1/2$ teaspoon minced garlic**
- ☐ **4 lamb noisettes**

Combine mustard, rosemary leaves and garlic. Spread mustard mixture over both sides of noisettes. Place under a preheated grill and cook for 5 minutes each side or until cooked as desired.

Serving suggestion: Crusty bread with boiled or steamed baby carrots and broccoli are easy accompaniments for this tasty main meal.

Cook's tip: A noisette is a small round steak, usually of lamb. The word literally means 'hazelnut' in French, signifying the roundness and meatiness of the particular cut. Because the cut is so tender, it cooks very quickly.

CUSTARD TART

Serves 8
Oven temperature 190°C, 375°F, Gas 5

- ☐ **125 mL (4 fl oz) sugar**
- ☐ **185 mL (6 fl oz) water**
- ☐ **3 eggs**
- ☐ **3 tablespoons milk**
- ☐ **1 x 23 cm (9 in) prepared sweet shortcrust pastry shell**
- ☐ **ground nutmeg**

1 Combine sugar and water in a saucepan and cook over a low heat, stirring constantly, for 4-5 minutes or until sugar dissolves. Set aside and allow to cool.
2 Place sugar syrup, eggs and milk in a mixing bowl and stir until combined. Pour into pastry shell and bake for 10 minutes. Reduce heat to 180°C (375°F/Gas 5) and bake for 20 minutes longer or until custard is firm.

Serving suggestion: Delicious hot, warm or cold sprinkled with nutmeg.

SHOPPING LIST
- ☐ 4 lamb noisettes
- ☐ fresh rosemary
- ☐ 1 x 23 cm (9 in) prepared sweet shortcrust pastry shell

PANTRY CHECK
- ☐ minced garlic
- ☐ wholegrain mustard
- ☐ ground nutmeg

MENU PLANNER
- ☐ Prepare and cook Custard Tart.
- ☐ Meanwhile, prepare and cook vegetables of your choice to accompany the main meal.
- ☐ Prepare and cook Lamb Noisettes with Mustard and Rosemary.

FETTUCCINE WITH BACON AND CREAM

Serves 4

- ☐ **500 g (1 lb) dried fettuccine**
- ☐ **4 tablespoons grated Parmesan cheese**

BACON AND CREAM SAUCE
- ☐ **2 rashers bacon, trimmed and chopped**
- ☐ **4 spring onions, chopped**
- ☐ **125 mL (4 fl oz) cream**
- ☐ **125 mL (4 fl oz) chicken stock**
- ☐ **3 tablespoons chopped sun-dried tomatoes (optional)**

1   Cook fettuccine in boiling water in a large saucepan following packet directions. Drain and set aside to keep warm.
2   To make sauce, cook bacon in a large frying pan for 4-5 minutes or until crisp. Add spring onions, and cook for 1 minute longer. Stir in cream and stock, bring to the boil then reduce heat and simmer until reduced and thickened. Stir in sun-dried tomatoes and toss fettuccine in cream sauce. Sprinkle with Parmesan cheese and serve.
Serving suggestion: A crisp salad and crusty bread is all that is needed to finish this course.

CHOC CHIP CHOCOLATE CAKE

Serves 8
Oven temperature 180°C, 350°F, Gas 4

- ☐ **1 packet chocolate cake mix**
- ☐ **125 g (4 oz) chocolate chips**

1   Prepare cake mix following packet directions, then fold through chocolate chips.
2   Spoon into a greased and lined 20 cm (8 in) round or fluted cake tin and bake for 35-40 minutes or until cooked when tested with a skewer.
Serving suggestion: Hot, warm or cold and accompanied with strawberries and cream, this makes a quick and easy dessert.

Left: Fettuccine with Bacon and Cream, Choc Chip Chocolate Cake
Right: Crab and Blue Cheese Quiche, Liqueur Orange Salad

SHOPPING LIST
- ☐ 2 rashers bacon
- ☐ spring onions
- ☐ 125 mL (4 fl oz) cream
- ☐ sun-dried tomatoes (optional)
- ☐ 1 packet chocolate cake mix
- ☐ 125 g (4 oz) chocolate chips

PANTRY CHECK
- ☐ prepared chicken stock or stock cubes
- ☐ 500 g (1 lb) dried fettuccine

- ☐ Parmesan cheese

MENU PLANNER
- ☐ Prepare and cook Choc Chip Chocolate Cake.
- ☐ Prepare salad vegetables of your choice. Cover and chill.
- ☐ Cook fettuccine.
- ☐ Meanwhile, prepare and cook Bacon and Cream Sauce for fettuccine.

Menu 30

CRAB AND BLUE CHEESE QUICHE

Serves 4
Oven temperature 190°C, 375°F, Gas 5

- ☐ **200 g (6¹/2 oz) prepared or ready-rolled shortcrust pastry, thawed**
- ☐ **6 spring onions, chopped**
- ☐ **185 g (6 oz) canned crabmeat, drained**
- ☐ **100 g (3¹/2 oz) Danish Blue Cheese**
- ☐ **2 eggs**
- ☐ **185 mL (6 fl oz) double cream**
- ☐ **¹/4 teaspoon ground nutmeg**

1 Line a 20 cm (8 in) flan dish with pastry. Line pastry case with baking paper, fill with dried beans or uncooked rice and bake for 10 minutes. Remove paper and beans or rice, reduce heat to 180°C (350°F/Gas 4) and cook for 7 minutes longer.
2 Sprinkle spring onions over pastry, then top with crabmeat. Place cheese, eggs and cream in a food processor or blender and process to combine. Pour over crabmeat, sprinkle with nutmeg and bake at 180°C (350°F/Gas 4) for 30 minutes or until firm.
Serving suggestion: Accompany with a crisp salad and wholemeal rolls.

LIQUEUR ORANGE SALAD

Serves 4

- ☐ **2 tablespoons Cointreau (orange liqueur)**
- ☐ **3 tablespoons orange juice**
- ☐ **1 tablespoon lemon juice**
- ☐ **2 tablespoons apricot jam**
- ☐ **¹/2 teaspoon ground cinnamon**
- ☐ **1 tablespoon grated orange rind**
- ☐ **3 tablespoons caster sugar**
- ☐ **3 tablespoons water**
- ☐ **4 oranges, peeled and segmented**
- ☐ **375 g (12 oz) canned mandarin segments, drained**

1 Combine Cointreau, orange juice, lemon juice, jam, cinnamon, orange rind, sugar and water in a saucepan and cook over a medium heat for 3-4 minutes or until mixture boils, then reduce heat and simmer for 3 minutes. Remove from heat and cool to room temperature.
2 Arrange fruit segments on four individual serving plates and spoon over syrup.

SHOPPING LIST

- ☐ spring onions
- ☐ 185 g (6 oz) canned crabmeat
- ☐ 100 g (3¹/2 oz) Danish Blue Cheese
- ☐ 185 mL (6 fl oz) double cream
- ☐ orange juice
- ☐ 1 lemon
- ☐ 4 oranges
- ☐ 375 g (12 oz) canned mandarin segments

PANTRY CHECK

- ☐ ground nutmeg

- ☐ 200 g (6¹/2 oz) prepared or ready-rolled puff pastry
- ☐ apricot jam
- ☐ ground cinnamon
- ☐ caster sugar
- ☐ Cointreau

MENU PLANNER

- ☐ Prepare and cook Crab and Blue Cheese Quiche.
- ☐ Meanwhile, prepare and make up dessert.
- ☐ Prepare salad vegetables of your choice. Cover and chill.

Pies and Pastries

With a little know-how and the convenience of prepared pastry you can make delicious pies and pastries in minutes.

BRIOCHES WITH DEVILLED KIDNEYS

Serves 4

- ☐ **6 lamb kidneys**
- ☐ **15 g (¹/2 oz) butter**
- ☐ **1 onion, finely chopped**
- ☐ **3 tablespoons tomato sauce**
- ☐ **1 tablespoon tomato paste**
- ☐ **3 tablespoons chicken stock**
- ☐ **2 teaspoons Worcestershire sauce**
- ☐ **2-3 drops Tabasco sauce**
- ☐ **1 teaspoon brown sugar**
- ☐ **1 teaspoon finely chopped fresh basil**
- ☐ **freshly ground black pepper**
- ☐ **2 tablespoons finely chopped fresh parsley**
- ☐ **4 brioches**
- ☐ **3 tablespoons natural yogurt**

1   Place kidneys in a bowl of lightly salted water and set aside to soak for 5 minutes. Remove skins, cords and fat from kidneys. Chop kidneys finely and set aside.
2   Melt butter in a frying pan and cook onion over a medium heat for 4-5 minutes. Add kidneys to pan and cook for 2-3 minutes or until colour just changes.
3   Combine tomato sauce, tomato paste, stock, Worcestershire sauce, Tabasco sauce, brown sugar and basil. Pour into pan with kidneys and cook over a low heat for 2-3 minutes. Season to taste with black pepper and stir in parsley.
4   Warm brioches in oven for 5-10 minutes, then remove top and scoop out centre and discard. Remove pan from heat, stir in yogurt, and cook over a low heat for 1 minute longer. Spoon kidney mixture into brioche shells, replace tops and serve.

CRAB CORNISH PASTIES

Makes 6
Oven temperature 200°C, 400°F, Gas 6

- ☐ **500 g (1 lb) prepared or ready-rolled shortcrust pastry sheets, thawed**
- ☐ **1 potato, peeled and grated**
- ☐ **185 g (6 oz) canned crabmeat, drained**
- ☐ **2 teaspoons mayonnaise**
- ☐ **1¹/2 tablespoons sour cream**
- ☐ **2 tablespoons snipped fresh chives**
- ☐ **2 teaspoons chopped fresh dill**
- ☐ **1 teaspoon lemon juice**
- ☐ **1-2 drops Tabasco sauce**
- ☐ **freshly ground black pepper**
- ☐ **1 egg, lightly beaten**

1   Cut six 13 cm (5 in) circles from pastry, using an upturned saucer as a guide and set aside.
2   Place potato, crabmeat, mayonnaise, sour cream, chives, dill, lemon juice and Tabasco sauce in a bowl and mix well to combine. Season to taste with black pepper.
3   Divide mixture into six equal portions and place a portion of crab mixture in the centre of each pastry round. Brush pastry edges with egg. Draw edges together over top of filling. Press to seal and crimp edges to make a fluted pattern. Brush with a little egg. Place onto a greased baking tray and bake for 25-30 minutes or until golden brown. Serve warm.

From left: Brioches with Devilled Kidneys, Quick Chicken Pies, Crab Cornish Pasties, Chicken Waldorf Mille Feuille

QUICK CHICKEN PIES

Serves 4
Oven temperature 200°C, 400°F, Gas 6

- [ ] **15 g (1 oz) butter**
- [ ] **125 g (4 oz) button mushrooms, sliced**
- [ ] **3 spring onions, finely chopped**
- [ ] **1 tablespoon sweet sherry**
- [ ] **440 g (14 oz) canned cream of mushroom soup**
- [ ] **125 mL (4 fl oz) milk**
- [ ] **1/2 teaspoon French mustard**
- [ ] **pinch cayenne pepper**
- [ ] **1 cooked chicken, flesh removed and chopped**
- [ ] **125 g (4 oz) sour cream**
- [ ] **4 x 150 mm (6 in) cooked vol-au-vent pastry cases**
- [ ] **2 tablespoons chopped fresh parsley**

1 Melt butter in a large frying pan and cook mushrooms and spring onions over a medium heat for 4-5 minutes or until mushrooms are soft.
2 Combine sherry, soup, milk, mustard and cayenne pepper, pour into pan with mushroom mixture. Cook over a low heat, stirring constantly, for 2 minutes. Bring to the boil, then remove pan from heat and stir in chicken and sour cream. Spoon mixture into vol-au-vent cases and bake for 15 minutes or until heated through. Sprinkle with parsley and serve.

CHICKEN WALDORF MILLE FEUILLE

Serves 4
Oven temperature 220°C, 425°F, Gas 7

- [ ] **200 g (6 1/2 oz) prepared and ready-rolled puff pastry, thawed**
- [ ] **1 egg, lightly beaten**
- [ ] **315 g (10 oz) cooked chopped chicken**
- [ ] **1 green apple, peeled, cored and thinly sliced**
- [ ] **2 stalks celery, sliced**
- [ ] **2 tablespoons sultanas**
- [ ] **3 tablespoons pecan nuts, roughly chopped**

BRANDY MAYONNAISE
- [ ] **3 tablespoons mayonnaise**
- [ ] **125 mL (4 fl oz) double cream**
- [ ] **1 tablespoon brandy**
- [ ] **pinch turmeric powder**
- [ ] **1/2 teaspoon Dijon mustard**
- [ ] **2 teaspoons chopped capers**
- [ ] **2 teaspoons snipped fresh chives**

1 Cut pastry into six rectangles each 8 x 13 cm (3 x 5 in). Place pastry rectangles on greased baking trays, then brush with egg and bake for 10-12 minutes or until golden brown. Remove from oven and cool on wire racks.
2 Place chicken, apple, celery, sultanas and pecan nuts in a bowl and mix to combine.
3 To make mayonnaise, place mayonnaise, cream, brandy, turmeric, mustard, capers and chives in a bowl and mix to combine. Pour mayonnaise over chicken mixture and toss to coat.
4 To assemble, cut pastry rectangles in half horizontally. Place a pastry rectangle on four individual serving dishes, top with half the chicken mixture, then another pastry layer. Repeat with remaining chicken mixture and pastry layer. Refrigerate until required.

Menu 31

FILLET OF PORK WITH MUSTARD CREAM

Serves 4

- ☐ **30 g (1 oz) butter**
- ☐ **2 onions, sliced**
- ☐ **500 g (1 lb) pork fillet, cut into thin strips**
- ☐ **1 tablespoon plain flour**
- ☐ **250 mL (8 fl oz) dry white wine**
- ☐ **1 tablespoon Dijon mustard**
- ☐ **125 mL (4 fl oz) double cream**
- ☐ **freshly ground black pepper**

1   Melt butter in a large frying pan and cook onions for 3-4 minutes or until soft, remove from pan and set aside. Add pork and cook in batches for 5 minutes or until pork is tender.

2   Return onions and pork to pan, then stir in flour and cook for 1 minute longer. Gradually stir in wine, mixing until well blended. Add mustard and cook over a medium heat, stirring constantly, until sauce boils and thickens. Stir in cream and black pepper to taste and cook gently for 4-5 minutes or until heated through.

Serving suggestion: Buttered noodles and steamed, or drained canned, asparagus complete this main meal.

PUFFED PRUNE WHIP

Serves 4
Oven temperature 180°C, 350°F, Gas 4

- ☐ **300 g (9¹/₂ oz) pitted prunes**
- ☐ **2 tablespoons icing sugar**
- ☐ **2 tablespoons Cointreau or orange juice**
- ☐ **2 teaspoons grated orange rind**
- ☐ **60 g (2 oz) chopped walnuts**
- ☐ **45 g (1¹/₂ oz) cake crumbs, finely processed**
- ☐ **4 egg whites**
- ☐ **3 tablespoons caster sugar**

1   Place prunes, icing sugar, Cointreau or orange juice, and orange rind in a food processor or blender and process until smooth. Transfer to a bowl and stir in walnuts and cake crumbs.

2   Beat egg whites until soft peaks form, then gradually add sugar, beating well after each addition. Continue beating until mixture is thick and glossy.

3   Fold egg white mixture into prune mixture. Spoon into a greased 18 cm (6 in) soufflé dish and cook for 25 minutes or until golden. Dust with icing sugar and serve.

SHOPPING LIST

- ☐ 500 g (1 lb) pork fillet, cut strips
- ☐ 2 onions
- ☐ 1 orange
- ☐ 125 mL (4 fl oz) double cream
- ☐ 300 g (9¹/₂ oz) pitted prunes
- ☐ 60 g (2 oz) walnuts

PANTRY CHECK

- ☐ dry white wine
- ☐ Dijon mustard
- ☐ Cointreau (optional)
- ☐ icing sugar
- ☐ caster sugar
- ☐ leftover cake to make 45 g (1¹/₂ oz) cake crumbs

MENU PLANNER

- ☐ Prepare and bake Puffed Prune Whip.
- ☐ Cook noodles.
- ☐ Prepare and cook Fillet of Pork with Mustard Cream.
- ☐ Meanwhile, prepare and cook fresh asparagus until tender, or heat drained, canned asparagus to accompany the main meal.

Menu 32

CHILLI CHICKEN

Serves 4
Oven temperature 220°C, 425°F, Gas 7

- ☐ **2 teaspoons minced ginger**
- ☐ **1 teaspoon minced garlic**
- ☐ **2 tablespoons honey**
- ☐ **2 teaspoons chilli sauce**
- ☐ **2 tablespoons lemon juice**
- ☐ **2 tablespoons soy sauce**
- ☐ **8 chicken thighs**

1 Place ginger, garlic, honey, chilli sauce, lemon juice and soy sauce in a bowl and mix well.
2 Brush chicken generously with mixture and place in a greased baking dish. Cook for 30 minutes or until chicken is cooked through and skin is crispy, basting frequently with sauce during cooking.
Serving suggestion: New potatoes, broccoli and carrots are an ideal accompaniment for this dish.

ICED SCOTTISH CREAM

Serves 4

- ☐ **4 egg yolks**
- ☐ **4 tablespoons honey, warmed**
- ☐ **300 mL (9¹/₂ oz) double cream**
- ☐ **2 tablespoons whisky**

1 Place egg yolks and honey in a mixing bowl and beat until thick and creamy.
2 Beat cream until soft peaks form, adding whisky gradually. Fold into honey mixture and spoon into four individual 125 mL (4 fl oz) capacity soufflé dishes. Cover and freeze.

Left: Fillet of Pork with Mustard Cream, Puffed Prune Whip
Below: Chilli Chicken, Iced Scottish Cream

SHOPPING LIST
- ☐ 8 chicken thighs
- ☐ chilli sauce
- ☐ 1 lemon
- ☐ 300 mL (9¹/₂ oz) double cream

PANTRY CHECK
- ☐ minced garlic
- ☐ minced ginger
- ☐ honey
- ☐ soy sauce
- ☐ whisky

MENU PLANNER
- ☐ Prepare and make up Iced Scottish Cream. Cover and freeze.
- ☐ Prepare and cook Chilli Chicken.
- ☐ Meanwhile, prepare and cook vegetables to accompany the main meal.

Menu 33

VEGETABLES IN GINGER ORANGE SAUCE

Serves 4

- [ ] **45 g (1¹/₂ oz) butter**
- [ ] **2 onions, cut into eighths**
- [ ] **1 teaspoon minced garlic**
- [ ] **2 teaspoons minced ginger**
- [ ] **1 teaspoon ground coriander**
- [ ] **1 large parsnip, peeled and cubed**
- [ ] **2 large turnips, peeled and cubed**
- [ ] **1 large carrot, peeled and cut into 1 cm (¹/₂ in) rounds**
- [ ] **1 sweet potato, cut into chunks**
- [ ] **6 new potatoes, peeled**
- [ ] **375 mL (12 fl oz) orange juice**
- [ ] **250 mL (8 fl oz) vegetable stock**
- [ ] **3 teaspoons cornflour blended with 3 tablespoons water**
- [ ] **freshly ground black pepper**
- [ ] **1 leek, chopped**
- [ ] **2 tablespoons snipped fresh chives**
- [ ] **1 tablespoon finely sliced orange rind**

1   Melt butter in a large saucepan and cook onion and garlic for 3-4 minutes or until onion is soft. Stir in ginger and coriander and cook for 1 minute longer.

2   Add parsnip, turnips, carrot, sweet potato, new potatoes, orange juice and stock. Cover, bring to the boil, then reduce heat and simmer for 25 minutes or until vegetables are tender. Remove vegetables using a slotted spoon and set aside.

3   Stir cornflour mixture into liquid and season to taste with black pepper. Bring to the boil and boil for 5 minutes, or until sauce thickens. Return vegetables to pan, with leek, chives and orange rind. Cook for 5 minutes longer or until heated through.

CHOCOLATE ROLL WITH RASPBERRY SAUCE

Serves 6

- [ ] **1 prepared chocolate Swiss roll**

RASPBERRY SAUCE
- [ ] **440 g (14 oz) canned raspberries, drained**
- [ ] **2 tablespoons raspberry liqueur (optional)**

1   To make sauce, place raspberries and raspberry liqueur, if using, in a food processor or blender and process until puréed. Push through a sieve to remove seeds.

2   Cut Swiss roll into slices and spoon over Raspberry Sauce.

SHOPPING LIST

- [ ] 2 onions
- [ ] 1 large parsnip
- [ ] 2 large turnips
- [ ] 1 large carrot
- [ ] 1 sweet potato
- [ ] 6 new potatoes
- [ ] 1 leek
- [ ] fresh chives
- [ ] 1 orange
- [ ] 375 mL (12 fl oz) orange juice
- [ ] 1 prepared chocolate Swiss roll
- [ ] 440 g (14 oz) canned raspberries

PANTRY CHECK

- [ ] minced garlic
- [ ] minced ginger
- [ ] ground coriander
- [ ] prepared vegetable stock or stock cube
- [ ] cornflour
- [ ] raspberry liqueur (optional)

MENU PLANNER

- [ ] Prepare and cook Vegetables in Ginger Orange Sauce.
- [ ] Meanwhile, prepare and make up Raspberry Sauce to go with chocolate roll.

Menu 34

LAMB IN MUSHROOM SAUCE

Serves 4

- ☐ **1 tablespoon oil**
- ☐ **1 onion, sliced**
- ☐ **500 g (1 lb) lean lamb, cut into thin strips**
- ☐ **250 g (8 oz) button mushrooms, sliced**
- ☐ **3 tablespoons sour cream**
- ☐ **3 tablespoons cream**
- ☐ **2 tablespoons tomato paste**
- ☐ **2 teaspoons ground rosemary**
- ☐ **1 teaspoon paprika**

1　Heat oil in a large frying pan and cook onion over a medium heat for 3-4 minutes or until soft. Add lamb and cook for 2-3 minutes or until browned. Add mushrooms and cook for 3 minutes longer.

2　Stir in sour cream, cream, tomato paste, rosemary and paprika and cook over a low heat without boiling for 4-5 minutes.

APPLE ALMOND TARTS

Serves 4

Oven temperature 190°C, 375°F, Gas 5

- ☐ **375 g (12 oz) prepared or ready-rolled shortcrust pastry, thawed**
- ☐ **250 mL (8 fl oz) canned apple sauce**
- ☐ **2 egg yolks, lightly beaten**
- ☐ **2 tablespoons honey**
- ☐ **3 tablespoons ground almonds**
- ☐ **1/2 teaspoon ground nutmeg**
- ☐ **2 large green apples, peeled, cored and finely sliced**
- ☐ **3 tablespoons lime marmalade, warmed**

1　Line four 10 cm (4 in) flan tins with pastry. Line with baking paper, and fill with dried beans or uncooked rice. Bake for 10 minutes then remove beans or rice and paper.

2　Place apple sauce, egg yolks, honey, almonds and nutmeg in a bowl and mix well. Spoon apple mixture into pastry cases and arrange apple slices over top.

3　Reduce oven temperature to 180°C (350°F, Gas 4) and bake for 20 minutes or until cooked through. Brush with melted marmalade.

Serving suggestion: Delicious served hot, warm or cold with whipped cream.

Left: Vegetables in Ginger Orange Sauce, Chocolate Roll with Raspberry Sauce
Above: Lamb in Mushroom Sauce, Apple Almond Tarts

Menu 35

STIR-FRY CHICKEN LIVERS WITH VEGETABLES

Serves 4

- ☐ **2 tablespoons olive oil**
- ☐ **1 onion, sliced**
- ☐ **1 teaspoon minced garlic**
- ☐ **500 g (1 lb) chicken livers, cut into thin strips**
- ☐ **1 tablespoon plain flour**
- ☐ **4 tablespoons dry sherry**
- ☐ **1 tablespoon caster sugar**
- ☐ **125 mL (4 fl oz) chicken stock**
- ☐ **1 large carrot, cut into thin strips**
- ☐ **freshly ground black pepper**
- ☐ **1 red pepper, cut into thin strips**
- ☐ **4 tablespoons bean sprouts**
- ☐ **3 spring onions, cut into thin strips**

1   Heat oil in a large frying pan and cook onion and garlic for 3-4 minutes or until onion is soft.
2   Place livers and flour in a plastic food bag and shake to coat livers. Add livers to pan and stir-fry for 2 minutes. Increase heat, stir in sherry and sugar and cook for 1 minute longer. Stir in stock, carrot and black pepper to taste. Cook for 1 minute.

Add red pepper, bean sprouts and spring onions, toss, and stir-fry for 2-3 minutes or until heated through. Serve immediately.
Serving suggestion: Serve on rice.

APRICOT SLICE WITH BRANDY CUSTARD

Serves 4
Oven temperature 180°C, 350°F, Gas 4

- ☐ **1 packet scone dough mix**
- ☐ **1 teaspoon mixed spice**
- ☐ **90 g (3 oz) finely chopped dried apricots, soaked and drained**

BRANDY CUSTARD
- ☐ **315 mL (10 fl oz) prepared vanilla custard**
- ☐ **4 tablespoons double cream**
- ☐ **2 tablespoons brandy**

1   Prepare scone dough following packet directions, adding mixed spice and apricots to dry ingredients before adding liquid.
2   Place dough into a greased and lined 18 x 28 cm (7 x 11¼ in) shallow cake pan and bake for 30 minutes or until cooked.
3   To make custard, combine custard, cream and brandy. Serve with apricot slice.

Menu 36

APPLE AND BLACKCURRANT CRUMBLE

Serves 4
Oven temperature 180°C, 350°F, Gas 4

- ☐ **440 g (14 oz) canned apple slices, drained and roughly chopped**
- ☐ **440 g (14 oz) canned blackcurrants, drained**

HAZELNUT TOPPING
- ☐ **125 g (4 oz) plain flour, sifted**
- ☐ **4 tablespoons brown sugar**
- ☐ **125 g (4 oz) chopped hazelnuts**
- ☐ **125 g (4 oz) butter, cut into small cubes**

1   Arrange apples and blackcurrants in an ovenproof dish.
2   To make topping, place flour, sugar, hazelnuts and butter in a food processor or blender and process until mixture resembles fine breadcrumbs. Sprinkle topping over fruit and bake for 15 minutes.

POTATO CURRY

Serves 4

- [ ] **2 tablespoons oil**
- [ ] **2 onions, sliced**
- [ ] **1 teaspoon minced garlic**
- [ ] **1 small aubergine, cubed**
- [ ] **2 large potatoes, cubed**
- [ ] **440 g (14 oz) canned peeled tomatoes, drained and chopped**
- [ ] **90 g (3 oz) frozen peas**
- [ ] **1 tablespoon tomato paste**
- [ ] **1 tablespoon mild curry powder**
- [ ] **2 teaspoons ground cumin**
- [ ] **2 teaspoons ground coriander**
- [ ] **250 mL (8 fl oz) coconut milk**
- [ ] **1 tablespoon lemon juice**

1   Heat oil in a large frying pan and cook onions, garlic, aubergine and potatoes over a medium heat, stirring constantly, for 2 minutes.

2   Stir in tomatoes, peas, tomato paste, curry powder, cumin, coriander and coconut milk, bring to simmering and simmer for 15 minutes or until vegetables are tender. Stir in lemon juice and serve.

Serving suggestion: Accompany with boiled rice and a salad.

Left: Stir-Fry Chicken Livers with Vegetables, Apricot Slice with Brandy Custard
Above: Potato Curry, Apple and Blackcurrant Crumble

Quick glazes

These easy glazes add flavour and interest to chops, steaks, chicken pieces, kebabs or fish fillets. Allow the food to marinate for 30 minutes if you have enough time.

ORIENTAL GLAZE
- [ ] **1 tablespoon teriyaki sauce**
- [ ] **2 tablespoons honey**
- [ ] **1 teaspoon hoisin sauce**
- [ ] **2 tablespoons tomato sauce**
- [ ] **1/4 teaspoon ground cumin**

1 Place teriyaki sauce, honey, hoisin sauce, tomato sauce and cumin in a bowl and mix to combine.
2 Brush meat, chicken or fish with glaze and grill, barbecue or bake.
Uses: Brushed over steaks, chops or ribs during cooking this glaze adds a spicy flavour reminiscent of the Orient. It can also be used as a sauce for a stir-fry of meat and vegetables.

ORANGE AND MINT GLAZE
- [ ] **125 mL (4 fl oz) orange juice**
- [ ] **1 teaspoon French mustard**
- [ ] **1 tablespoon honey**
- [ ] **2 tablespoons mint jelly, warmed**

1 Place orange juice, mustard, honey and mint jelly in a bowl and mix to combine.
2 Brush over meat and grill, barbecue, pan cook or bake.
Uses: Delicious used on pork, veal or lamb. Add extra flavour to a lamb roast by basting with this glaze during the last 30 minutes of cooking.

SATAY GLAZE
- [ ] **2 teaspoons brown sugar**
- [ ] **1 teaspoon soy sauce**
- [ ] **1 tablespoon oyster sauce**
- [ ] **1 tablespoon dry sherry**
- [ ] **1 tablespoon peanut butter**
- [ ] **3 tablespoons water**

1 Place sugar, soy sauce, oyster sauce, sherry, peanut butter and water in a bowl and mix to combine.

2 Brush meat, poultry or fish with glaze and grill, barbecue, pan cook or bake.
Uses: Brush over kebabs for an added flavour boost. Or use as a sauce for stir-fry beef or lamb with onions. Stir in glaze just before serving.

APRICOT GLAZE
- [ ] **125 g (4 oz) apricot jam, warmed**
- [ ] **3 tablespoons teriyaki sauce**
- [ ] **1 clove garlic, crushed**
- [ ] **1/2 teaspoon ground mixed spice**
- [ ] **1 tablespoon cider vinegar**

1 Place jam, teriyaki sauce, garlic, mixed spice and vinegar in a bowl and mix to combine.
2 Brush glaze over meat, chicken or fish and grill, barbecue, pan cook or bake.
Uses: For a quick, easy and delicious meal, try this glaze brushed over ham steaks or chicken fillets.

LEMON, CHILLI AND GINGER GLAZE
- [ ] **2 tablespoons olive oil**
- [ ] **2 tablespoons lemon juice**
- [ ] **2 teaspoons wholegrain mustard**
- [ ] **2 tablespoons ginger marmalade**
- [ ] **1 teaspoon minced chilli**
- [ ] **2 tablespoons finely chopped fresh coriander**

1 Place oil, lemon juice, mustard, marmalade, chilli and coriander in a bowl and mix to combine.
2 Brush glaze over meat, chicken or fish and grill, barbecue, pan cook or bake.
Uses: For a quick meal with a difference, place a piece of fish in aluminium foil, spoon over some glaze, dot with butter, enclose foil and bake, grill or barbecue.

Use these glazes to add flavour and interest to meat, chicken or fish

Weekday winners

Although these meals take a little longer to prepare, they are well worth the wait. Surprise and delight your family and friends with homebaked Steak Pie prepared and served in under an hour.

Menu 37

CITRUS CRUSTED LAMB RACKS

Serves 6
Oven temperature 180°C, 350°F, Gas 4

- ☐ **3 racks of lamb, each containing 6 cutlets**
- ☐ **1$^1/_2$ tablespoons wholegrain mustard**
- ☐ **4 tablespoons lime marmalade**
- ☐ **30 g (1 oz) breadcrumbs, made from stale bread**
- ☐ **1 teaspoon minced ginger**
- ☐ **2 tablespoons chopped fresh parsley**
- ☐ **$^1/_4$ teaspoon ground cardamom**
- ☐ **2 teaspoons brown sugar**
- ☐ **2 teaspoons grated lime rind**
- ☐ **1$^1/_2$ tablespoons lime juice**
- ☐ **30 g (1 oz) butter, melted**

1 Trim meat of all visible fat. Combine mustard and marmalade and spread over meat.
2 Place breadcrumbs, ginger, parsley, cardamom, brown sugar, lime rind, lime juice and butter in a bowl and mix well to combine. Press half the mixture onto the back of each rack and bake for 45 minutes. Stand for 5 minutes before serving.
Serving suggestion: Accompany with green peas and new potatoes.

Citrus Crusted Lamb Racks, Apple Sponge Dessert

APPLE SPONGE DESSERT

Serves 6
Oven temperature 180°C, 350°F, Gas 4

- ☐ **1 packet sponge cake mix**
- ☐ **440 g (14 oz) canned apple slices**
- ☐ **3 tablespoons sultanas**
- ☐ **2 teaspoons grated lemon rind**
- ☐ **2 tablespoons honey, warmed**
- ☐ **1 tablespoon lemon juice**
- ☐ **icing sugar**

1 Make up cake mix following packet instructions.
2 Place apples, sultanas, lemon rind, honey and lemon juice in a bowl and mix to combine.
3 Spread apple mixture over the base of a greased ovenproof dish, top with cake mix. Bake for 35-40 minutes or until golden. Just prior to serving dust with icing sugar.

SHOPPING LIST
- ☐ 3 racks lamb, each containing 6 cutlets
- ☐ fresh parsley
- ☐ 1 lime
- ☐ 1 lemon
- ☐ 440 g (14 oz) canned apple slices
- ☐ 1 packet sponge cake mix
- ☐ brown sugar
- ☐ sultanas
- ☐ honey
- ☐ icing sugar

PANTRY CHECK
- ☐ wholegrain mustard
- ☐ lime marmalade
- ☐ minced ginger
- ☐ ground cardamom

MENU PLANNER
- ☐ Prepare and cook Citrus Crusted Lamb Racks.
- ☐ Meanwhile, make up and cook Apple Sponge Dessert.
- ☐ Boil, steam or microwave potatoes.
- ☐ Boil, steam or microwave squash and peas separately.

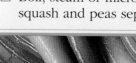

SHOPPING LIST

- [ ] 4 slices topside beef, each 1 cm (¹/₂ in) thick
- [ ] spinach
- [ ] 2 carrots
- [ ] 185 mL (6 fl oz) double cream
- [ ] mixed peel

PANTRY CHECK

- [ ] minced garlic
- [ ] white wine
- [ ] caster sugar
- [ ] orange marmalade
- [ ] icing sugar

MENU PLANNER

- [ ] Prepare and cook Marmalade Bread Pudding.
- [ ] Meanwhile, prepare and cook rolls.
- [ ] Prepare vegetables.
- [ ] Cook rice and vegetables.

BEEF AND SPINACH ROLLS

Serves 4

- [ ] **4 spinach leaves**
- [ ] **2 carrots, peeled and cut into 5 mm x 20 cm (¹/₄ x 8 in) sticks**
- [ ] **4 slices topside beef, each 1 cm (¹/₂ in) thick**
- [ ] **freshly ground black pepper**
- [ ] **155 g (5 oz) butter**
- [ ] **¹/₂ teaspoon minced garlic**
- [ ] **125 mL (4 fl oz) white wine**
- [ ] **2 teaspoons caster sugar**

1   Remove stalks from spinach and cut leaves into 2 pieces. Blanch leaves in the microwave for 30 seconds, or in a saucepan of boiling water for 1 minute. Drain. Blanch carrot sticks in the microwave for 1 minute, or in a saucepan of boiling water for 2 minutes. Refresh under cold water. Drain.

2   Pound beef into thin slices, using a meat tenderiser. Place a spinach leaf on each slice of beef, then 5-6 carrot strips and season to taste with black pepper. Roll up tightly and secure with toothpicks.

3   Melt butter with garlic in a large frying pan over a medium heat. Add beef rolls and cook until golden. Add wine and sugar to pan, cover and simmer for 10-12 minutes or until meat is cooked.

Serving suggestion: Slice rolls, place on a bed of brown rice and spoon over sauce. Accompany with a green vegetable such as beans.

MARMALADE BREAD PUDDING

Serves 4
Oven temperature 180°C, 350°F, Gas 4

- [ ] **16 slices white bread**
- [ ] **60 g (2 oz) butter, softened**
- [ ] **4 tablespoons orange marmalade**
- [ ] **2 tablespoons mixed peel**
- [ ] **4 eggs, lightly beaten**
- [ ] **3 tablespoons icing sugar**
- [ ] **315 mL (10 fl oz) milk**
- [ ] **185 mL (6 fl oz) double cream**
- [ ] **2 tablespoons sugar**

1   Using bread, butter and marmalade, make 8 sandwiches. Remove crusts and cut each sandwich into 9 squares. Place bread cubes into a lightly buttered, deep-sided, ovenproof dish and sprinkle with mixed peel.

2   Place eggs, icing sugar, milk and cream in a bowl and whisk to combine. Slowly pour egg mixture over bread, allowing it to be absorbed.

3   Sprinkle sugar over top of pudding and bake for 45 minutes.

Serving suggestion: Dust top of pudding with icing sugar and serve hot or warm.

Left: Beef and Spinach Rolls, Marmalade Bread Pudding
Right: Gourmet Lentil Burgers, Fruit Squares

Menu 39

GOURMET
LENTIL BURGERS

Serves 4

- ☐ **90g (3 oz) red lentils, cooked, drained and mashed**
- ☐ **125 g (4 oz) instant mashed potato**
- ☐ **185 mL (6 fl oz) milk**
- ☐ **1 egg, lightly beaten**
- ☐ **4 spring onions, finely chopped**
- ☐ **1/2 teaspoon minced garlic**
- ☐ **1 teaspoon ground cumin**
- ☐ **1 tablespoon finely chopped fresh coriander**
- ☐ **1 teaspoon curry powder**
- ☐ **freshly ground black pepper**
- ☐ **4 bread rolls, split and toasted**

YOGURT MINT SAUCE
- ☐ **250 g (8 oz) natural yogurt**
- ☐ **1 tablespoon chopped fresh mint**

1   Place lentils, mashed potato, milk, egg, spring onions, garlic, cumin, coriander, curry powder and black pepper to taste in a bowl and mix well.

2   Shape lentil mixture into eight patties and cook under a preheated grill for 5 minutes each side or until golden and heated through.

3   To make sauce, place yogurt and mint in a bowl and mix to combine. Place two patties on the bottom half of each bread roll, then top with sauce.

Serving suggestion: Accompany with carrot ribbons, cucumber slices, onion rings, sliced tomatoes and alfalfa sprouts.

FRUIT SQUARES

Serves 4
Oven temperature 180°C, 350°F, Gas 4

- ☐ **250 g (8 oz) butter**
- ☐ **90 g (3 oz) brown sugar**
- ☐ **185 g (6 oz) plain flour, sifted with 1 teaspooon baking powder**
- ☐ **125 g (4 oz) rolled oats**
- ☐ **3 tablespoons chopped walnuts**
- ☐ **500 g (1 lb) bottled mincemeat**

1   Place butter and sugar in a food processor and process until light and creamy. Add flour mixture, oats and walnuts and process to combine.

2   Pat half the mixture into a greased and lined 23 cm (9 in) square shallow cake tin. Top with mincemeat, then cover with remaining oat mixture. Bake for 40 minutes.

Serving suggestion: Serve hot, warm or cold, cut into squares, with whipped cream.

Menu 40

SHOPPING LIST
- ☐ 750 g (1¹/₂ lb) lean minced steak
- ☐ 1 onion

PANTRY CHECK
- ☐ 750 g (1¹/₂ lb) prepared or shortcrust pastry
- ☐ tomato purée
- ☐ tomato paste
- ☐ Worcestershire sauce
- ☐ prepared beef stock or stock cubes

MENU PLANNER
- ☐ Prepare and cook Steak Pie.
- ☐ Meanwhile, prepare and cook vegetables.

STEAK PIE

Serves 4
Oven temperature 190°C, 375°F, Gas 5

- ☐ **750 g (1¹/₂ lb) prepared or ready-rolled shortcrust pastry, thawed**
- ☐ **30 g (1 oz) butter, melted**

MEAT FILLING
- ☐ **30 g (1 oz) butter**
- ☐ **1 onion, chopped**
- ☐ **750 g (1¹/₂ lb) lean minced steak**
- ☐ **2 tablespoons plain flour**
- ☐ **125 g (4 oz) tomato purée**
- ☐ **1 tablespoon tomato paste**
- ☐ **2 tablespoons Worcestershire sauce**
- ☐ **170 mL (5¹/₂ fl oz) beef stock**

1 To make filling, melt butter in a frying pan and cook onion for 3-4 minutes or until soft. Add minced steak and cook until brown. Stir in flour and cook for 1 minute longer. Combine tomato purée, tomato paste, Worcestershire sauce and stock and stir into pan. Bring to boil, stirring constantly, then reduce heat and simmer, uncovered for 5 minutes, or until most of the liquid has evaporated and mixture thickens. Set aside to cool.

2 Line a 23 cm (9 in) pie dish using three-quarters of the pastry and brush edges with water. Spoon meat filling over pastry. Cover meat with remaining pastry and press edges together. Pinch edges with fingertips to make a decorative edge and make a slit in centre of pastry. Bake for 20 minutes or until golden brown.

Serving suggestion: Accompany pie with mashed potatoes and peas or green beans.

Above: Steak Pie
Right: Layered Ham and Cheese Bake, Lemon Syllabubs

Menu 41

LAYERED HAM AND CHEESE BAKE

Serves 4
Oven temperature 200°C, 400°F, Gas 6

- [ ] **4 eggs**
- [ ] **170 mL (5¹/₂ fl oz) milk**
- [ ] **8 slices wholemeal bread, cut into quarters**
- [ ] **125 g (4 oz) ham, chopped**
- [ ] **4 tablespoons finely chopped red pepper**
- [ ] **6 spring onions, chopped**
- [ ] **125 g (4 oz) grated Cheddar cheese**

1 Place eggs and milk in a mixing bowl and whisk until combined. Brush bread with egg mixture. Combine ham, red pepper and spring onions.

2 Place 4 slices of bread into a lightly greased ovenproof dish, top with half the ham mixture and sprinkle with half the cheese. Repeat layers with remaining ingredients. Pour over any remaining egg mixture and bake for 30 minutes or until firm and top is golden brown.

Serving suggestion: To complete this tasty meal, accompany the bake with a stir-fry of vegetables such as mangetout, sliced onions, sliced carrots, pepper strips and celery sticks.

LEMON SYLLABUBS

Serves 4

- [ ] **2 tablespoons lemon juice**
- [ ] **125 mL (4 fl oz) white wine**
- [ ] **3 tablespoons caster sugar**
- [ ] **250 mL (8 fl oz) double cream**
- [ ] **2 lemon slices, quartered**

Place lemon juice, white wine, caster sugar and cream in a bowl and beat until soft peaks form. Spoon into four individual serving glasses and decorate with lemon slices.

Cook's tip: Always use freshly squeezed lemon juice in desserts. It has a more mellow flavour than packaged lemon juice.

HERB AND RICOTTA GNOCCHI

Serves 4

- [ ] **250 g (8 oz) ricotta cheese**
- [ ] **90 g (3 oz) instant mashed potato**
- [ ] **2 tablespoons chopped fresh parsley**
- [ ] **1 tablespoon chopped fresh basil**
- [ ] **60 g (2 oz) grated Parmesan cheese**
- [ ] **$^1/_4$ teaspoon ground nutmeg**
- [ ] **2 eggs, lightly beaten**
- [ ] **plain flour**

TOMATO SAUCE
- [ ] **440 g (14 oz) canned peeled tomatoes, drained, liquid reserved and seeds removed**
- [ ] **2 teaspoons sweet fruit chutney**
- [ ] **2 teaspoons tomato paste**
- [ ] **1 teaspoon minced garlic**

1   Place ricotta cheese, mashed potato, parsley, basil, Parmesan cheese, nutmeg and egg in a large bowl and mix to combine. Take tablespoons of mixture and roll into balls, then dust with flour.

2   To make sauce, place tomatoes, chutney, tomato paste and garlic in a food processor or blender and process to combine. Push through a sieve to remove seeds. Place sauce in a microwave-safe jug and cook on HIGH (100%) for 3 minutes or until heated through, or heat in a small saucepan over a medium heat.

3   Bring a large saucepan of water to the boil, then reduce heat so that the water is simmering. Drop gnocchi into simmering water and cook for 2 minutes or until they rise to the surface. Using a slotted spoon, remove gnocchi and drain on absorbent paper. Spoon sauce over gnocchi.

Herb and Ricotta Gnocchi, Walnut Whizz Cake

WALNUT WHIZZ CAKE

Serves 4
Oven temperature 180°C, 350°F, Gas 4

- [ ] **220 g (7 oz) caster sugar**
- [ ] **4 tablespoons plain flour**
- [ ] **90g (3 oz) desiccated coconut**
- [ ] **60 g (2 oz) chopped walnuts**
- [ ] **2 teaspoons grated lemon rind**
- [ ] **4 eggs**
- [ ] **375 mL (12 fl oz) milk**
- [ ] **125 g (4 oz) butter, melted**
- [ ] **250 mL (8 fl oz) double cream, whipped**

1   Place sugar, flour, coconut, walnuts and lemon rind in a food processor and process for 30 seconds. Add eggs, milk and butter and process for 1 minute longer.

2   Pour mixture into a greased and lined 23 cm (9 in) flan dish. Bake for 45 minutes or until cake is cooked when tested. Serve warm with whipped cream.

SHOPPING LIST
- [ ] 250 g (8 oz) ricotta cheese
- [ ] 90 g (3 oz) instant mashed potato
- [ ] fresh parsley
- [ ] fresh basil
- [ ] 1 lemon
- [ ] 250 mL (8 fl oz) double cream

PANTRY CHECK
- [ ] Parmesan cheese
- [ ] ground nutmeg
- [ ] 440 g (14 oz) canned peeled tomatoes
- [ ] sweet fruit chutney
- [ ] tomato paste
- [ ] minced garlic
- [ ] caster sugar
- [ ] desiccated coconut
- [ ] 60 g (2 oz) walnuts

MENU PLANNER
- [ ] Prepare and cook cake.
- [ ] Prepare gnocchi.
- [ ] Prepare and heat sauce for gnocchi.
- [ ] Cook gnocchi.

CAJUN HAMBURGERS WITH TOMATO RELISH

Serves 4

- ☐ **2 tablespoons ground black pepper**
- ☐ **2 teaspoons paprika**
- ☐ **4 beef medallions, each 3 cm (1¹/₂ in) thick**
- ☐ **1 tablespoon vegetable oil**
- ☐ **4 bread rolls, split and toasted**
- ☐ **4 large lettuce leaves**
- ☐ **4 tablespoons prepared pasta sauce or tomato relish**

1   Combine black pepper and paprika. Coat beef medallions with pepper mixture. Heat oil in a frying pan until it begins to smoke and cook medallions over a medium heat for 3-4 minutes each side or until cooked as desired. Place pasta sauce or relish in a small saucepan and cook over a medium heat until heated through.
2   Top the bottom half of each roll with a lettuce leaf, then a medallion and a spoonful of sauce or relish.

STICKY DATE PUDDING

Serves 4
Oven temperature 180°C, 350°F, Gas 4

- ☐ **250 g (8 oz) pitted, chopped dates**
- ☐ **1 packet sponge cake mix**

TOFFEE SYRUP
- ☐ **170 g (5¹/₂ oz) brown sugar**
- ☐ **4 tablespoons double cream**
- ☐ **125 g (4 oz) butter**
- ☐ **2 teaspoons vanilla essence**

1   Cover dates with boiling water and set aside while preparing rest of the pudding.
2   Make cake according to packet directions. Drain dates and fold through cake batter.
3   Spoon cake batter into a greased and lined 20 cm (8 in) springform tin and bake for 35-40 minutes, or until cooked.
4   To make syrup, combine sugar, cream, butter and vanilla in a small saucepan. Bring to the boil, over a low heat, then reduce heat and simmer for 2-3 minutes. Spoon one-third of toffee syrup over cooked pudding and return it to oven for 5 minutes.
Serving suggestion: Serve pudding with remaining syrup and whipped cream.

Above: Cajun Hamburgers with Tomato Relish, Sticky Date Pudding
Right: Parmesan Risotto, Apple Dessert Cake

SHOPPING LIST
- ☐ 4 beef medallions, each 3 cm (1¹/₂ in) thick
- ☐ 4 bread rolls
- ☐ 1 lettuce
- ☐ 250 g (8 oz) pitted dates
- ☐ 125 mL (4 fl oz) double cream
- ☐ prepared pasta sauce or tomato relish

PANTRY CHECK
- ☐ ground paprika
- ☐ 1 packet sponge cake mix
- ☐ brown sugar
- ☐ vanilla essence

MENU PLANNER
- ☐ Make and bake pudding.
- ☐ Prepare, cook and make up Cajun Hamburgers.

Menu 44

PARMESAN RISOTTO

Serves 4

- [ ] **2 tablespoons olive oil**
- [ ] **¹/₂ teaspoon minced garlic**
- [ ] **1 onion, peeled and chopped**
- [ ] **220 g (7 oz) short-grain white rice**
- [ ] **500 g (1 lb) peeled and grated carrots**
- [ ] **¹/₄ teaspoon ground turmeric**
- [ ] **125 mL (4 fl oz) dry white wine**
- [ ] **750 mL (1¹/₄ pt) chicken or vegetable stock**
- [ ] **¹/₂ red pepper, seeded and chopped**
- [ ] **90g (3 oz) grated Parmesan cheese**
- [ ] **2 spring onions, chopped**
- [ ] **freshly ground black pepper**

1   Heat oil in a large frying pan and cook garlic and onion for 3 minutes or until onion is soft. Reduce heat to low, stir in rice and carrots and cook, stirring for 3 minutes.
2   Combine turmeric and wine and pour into rice, bring to the boil, then reduce heat and simmer, stirring constantly, for 5 minutes or until liquid has been absorbed.
3   Stir 375 mL (12 fl oz) of stock into rice mixture. Bring to the boil, then reduce heat, cover and simmer for 10 minutes or until stock is absorbed. Add remaining stock and cook, stirring occasionally, for 25 minutes or until rice is cooked and most of the liquid is absorbed.
4   Stir in red pepper, Parmesan cheese, spring onions and black pepper to taste.

APPLE DESSERT CAKE

Serves 6
Oven temperature 160°C, 325°F, Gas 3

- [ ] **1 teaspoon ground mixed spice**
- [ ] **1 packet sponge cake mix**
- [ ] **45 g (1¹/₂ oz) desiccated coconut**
- [ ] **440 g (14 oz) canned apple slices, drained**
- [ ] **4 tablespoons apricot jam, melted**

1   Combine mixed spice with butter cake mix, then make up following packet directions. Fold in coconut.
2   Spoon half the cake mix into a lightly greased and lined 20 cm (8 in) round cake tin, top with half the apples and remaining cake mix. Arrange remaining apple slices.
3   Bake for 50-60 minutes or until cake is cooked when tested. Brush with jam.

SHOPPING LIST
- [ ] 750 g (1¹/₂ lb) carrots
- [ ] 1 onion
- [ ] 1 red pepper
- [ ] spring onions
- [ ] 440 g (14 oz) canned apple slices
- [ ] 1 packet sponge cake mix

PANTRY CHECK
- [ ] olive oil
- [ ] minced garlic
- [ ] short-grain rice
- [ ] ground turmeric

- [ ] dry white wine
- [ ] prepared vegetable or chicken stock or stock cubes
- [ ] Parmesan cheese
- [ ] ground mixed spice
- [ ] desiccated coconut
- [ ] apricot jam

MENU PLANNER
- [ ] Prepare and cook Apple Dessert Cake.
- [ ] Prepare and cook risotto.
- [ ] Brush top of Apple Dessert Cake with jam.

Operation deep-freeze

One of the quickest ways to provide quick meals is to cook ahead and freeze. To freeze meals successfully requires a little thought and planning.

☐ Choose containers and wrap that are easy to label and are nonporous, so flavours and odours do not escape.

☐ When purchasing containers, wrap or bags, make sure they are labelled freezer-safe.

☐ For best results, remove as much air as possible from the container before freezing. Vacuum pumps are available for this purpose.

☐ Air discolours food and causes dehydration, known as freezer-burn. This is evident when the food becomes discoloured, stringy and tasteless. Any food that suffers freezer-burn should be discarded.

☐ Clear labelling is essential when freezing. Some freezer bags have labels printed on them. Use either a waterproof felt pen or a wax pencil when labelling and mark with date and contents. Frozen food looks very different from fresh food, and in a

week, month or year you may not know what is in the packet or how long it has been there.

☐ When freezing liquids and cooked foods, always leave 2-3 cm (^{3}/$_4$-1^1/$_4$ in) headspace between the top of the food and the lid of the container. This allows for expansion of the food during freezing and will prevent overflows.

☐ To save time, cut meat and poultry into the portions you require before freezing. It is easier to take two packs from the freezer for extra people than to cook too much through overpacking.

☐ If meat and poultry is already in wrapping, remove wrapping and repack in a freezer bag or container before freezing.

☐ If you wish to

marinate frozen meat or poultry it can be placed in the marinade while still frozen so that thawing and marinating take place at the same time.

FREEZING COOKED FOODS

Cooking ahead and freezing is a real boon for those busier days. With a little planning, you can reduce the time spent shopping, preparing, cooking and washing-up. Eventually you will be able to turn to the freezer in place of the local deli or take-away when faced with an empty refrigerator or lack of menu inspiration.

☐ Most cooked food undergoes much less change in texture than raw food.

☐ Avoid dishes with egg-based sauces such as mayonnaise, as they tend to curdle when frozen.

☐ Garlic and onion in cooked food tends to lose flavour after three months.

☐ Some spices, such as cinnamon and nutmeg, only have a freezer life of two months.

☐ It is best to add potatoes to stews and casseroles when you reheat as they tend to lose their texture if stored longer than a month.

FOODS THAT DO NOT FREEZE SUCCESSFULLY

Eggs in their shells or hard-boiled – if frozen the whites toughen and become rubbery.

Emulsified sauces such as mayonnaise separate, however, this can be overcome by vigorous beating or by processing in a food processor or blender.

Soft meringues become tough and sticky.

Jellies lose their gloss and break down.

Potatoes in cooked foods such as casseroles become watery and lose flavour. If the dish has potatoes in it, add them when you reheat.

Raw salad vegetables, such as lettuce, tomatoes, celery, cucumber or radishes, wilt. Also avoid freezing sandwiches with these ingredients as fillings.

Sour cream, yogurt, cultured buttermilk, made-up dips and **curd style cottage cheese** are not recommended for freezing by the manufacturer, as texture changes on freezing.

Watermelon turns to mush when thawed.

FREEZER GUIDE

While food can be kept for longer than the times given below, these storage times will ensure that the food stays at its best.

Food	Freezer storage life
Beef	12 months
Lamb	9 months
Pork	6 months
Veal	9 months
Ham on the bone	3 months
Ham, sliced	1 month
Bacon rashers	1 month
Chicken	12 months
Turkey	6 months
Duck	12 months
Oily fish such as salmon, trout, mackerel	2 months
White fish	6 months
Shellfish	1 month
Casseroles	6 months
Curries	6 months
Soups	3 months
Stock	6-12 months

EATBALLS
_/ ı / 9ı

Time to please

Entertaining is one of the best ways to socialise and enjoy life, but no one wants to spend hours preparing for the occasion. These quick-to-prepare menus are ideal for those with more style than time.

Menu 45

STIR-FRY GARLIC MUSHROOMS

Serves 4

- ☐ **1 tablespoon olive oil**
- ☐ **45 g (1¹/₂ oz) butter**
- ☐ **1¹/₂ teaspoons minced garlic**
- ☐ **375 g (12 oz) button mushrooms, trimmed**
- ☐ **4 bacon rashers, chopped**
- ☐ **4 tablespoons breadcrumbs, made from stale bread**
- ☐ **2 tablespoons chopped fresh basil**
- ☐ **250 g (8 oz) bean sprouts**

Heat oil and butter in a large frying pan and cook garlic and mushrooms over a medium heat for 2-3 minutes. Add bacon and breadcrumbs and cook for 2 minutes longer. Stir in basil and serve on a bed of bean sprouts or with toast wedges.

LAMB GOULASH

Serves 4

- ☐ **2 tablespoons oil**
- ☐ **2 onions, sliced**
- ☐ **1 red pepper, sliced**
- ☐ **1 teaspoon minced garlic**
- ☐ **500g (1 lb) lamb strips**
- ☐ **4 tablespoons plain flour**
- ☐ **1 tablespoon paprika**
- ☐ **440 g (14 oz) canned peeled tomatoes, undrained and mashed**
- ☐ **250 mL (8 fl oz) beef stock**
- ☐ **125 mL (4 fl oz) sour cream**
- ☐ **1 tablespoon caraway seeds**

1   Heat 1 tablespoon oil in a frying pan and cook onions, red pepper and garlic for 4-5 minutes or until onion is soft. Remove from pan and set aside.

2   Toss lamb in flour. Add remaining oil to pan and cook lamb in batches for 4-5 minutes or until brown. Return lamb to pan, stir in paprika and cook for 1 minute longer. Return onion mixture with tomatoes and beef stock to pan, bring to the boil, then reduce heat and simmer, uncovered, for 30 minutes.

3   Remove from heat, stir through sour cream and caraway seeds. Serve with rice, noodles or mashed potatoes.

SHOPPING LIST

- ☐ 500g (1 lb) lamb strips
- ☐ 375 g (12 oz) button mushrooms
- ☐ 4 rashers bacon
- ☐ fresh basil
- ☐ 250 g (8 oz) bean sprouts
- ☐ 1 red pepper
- ☐ 2 onions
- ☐ 1 large lemon
- ☐ 375 mL (12 fl oz) double cream
- ☐ 125 mL (4 fl oz) sour cream

PANTRY CHECK

- ☐ olive oil
- ☐ minced garlic
- ☐ paprika
- ☐ 440 g (14 oz) canned peeled tomatoes
- ☐ caraway seeds (optional)
- ☐ prepared beef stock or beef stock cubes
- ☐ gelatine
- ☐ caster sugar
- ☐ desiccated coconut

MENU PLANNER

Earlier in the day
- ☐ Make the Lemon Soufflés and refrigerate until required.
- ☐ Prepare and cook the Lamb Goulash up to step 3.

30 minutes before serving
- ☐ Prepare and cook stir-fry.
- ☐ Gently reheat the Lamb Goulash. Just prior to serving stir in soured cream and caraway seeds.
- ☐ Cook rice, noodles or potatoes.

LEMON SOUFFLES

Serves 4

- ☐ **3 eggs, separated**
- ☐ **2 tablespoons lemon juice**
- ☐ **3 tablespoons sugar**
- ☐ **200 mL (6^1/2 fl oz) double cream**
- ☐ **2 tablespoons gelatine dissolved in 4 tablespoons hot water and cooled**
- ☐ **4 tablespoons caster sugar**

TOPPING
- ☐ **125 mL (4 fl oz) double cream, whipped**
- ☐ **4 tablespoons desiccated coconut, toasted**
- ☐ **strips lemon rind**

1   Combine egg yolks, lemon juice and sugar in a bowl. Place over a saucepan of simmering water and cook, stirring constantly, until mixture thickens slightly. Remove bowl from saucepan and set aside to cool slightly.

2   Beat cream until soft peaks form. Fold into custard, then fold in cooled gelatine mixture. Beat egg whites until soft peaks form, then gradually add caster sugar and continue to beat until thick and glossy. Fold egg white mixture into custard mixture.

3   Cut four strips of greaseproof paper, long enough to wrap around four 250 mL (8 fl oz) capacity soufflé dishes and to extend 5 cm (2 in) above edge of dishes. Lightly grease paper then wrap around the outside of each dish and secure with string. Spoon mixture into dishes to come up approximately 1^1/2 cm (^{3}/4 in) above the rim of each dish. Chill for 2 hours or until set.

4   Decorate top of soufflés with a little whipped cream, desiccated coconut and strips of lemon rind.

Microwave hint: Sprinkle gelatine over 4 tablespoons cold water and microwave on HIGH (100%) for 20 seconds.

Stir-Fry Garlic Mushrooms, Lamb Goulash, Lemon Soufflés

Menu 46

CELERY AND CHEESE SOUP

Serves 4

- [ ] **30 g (1 oz) butter**
- [ ] **1 onion, chopped**
- [ ] **4 stalks celery, finely chopped**
- [ ] **1 tablespoon plain flour**
- [ ] **250 mL (8 fl oz) milk**
- [ ] **250 mL (8 fl oz) chicken stock**
- [ ] **60 g (2 oz) Stilton cheese**

1   Melt butter in a large saucepan and cook onion and celery over a medium heat for 3-4 minutes or until tender. Stir in flour and cook for 1 minute longer. Remove pan from heat and whisk in milk and stock a little at a time until well blended. Return to heat and bring to the boil, stirring constantly, until mixture thickens.

2   Reduce heat and simmer, covered, for 15 minutes. Add cheese and stir until melted.

Celery and Cheese Soup, Broccoli and Herb Quiche, Minted Green Salad, Butterscotch Crêpes

MINTED GREEN SALAD

Serves 4

- ☐ **125 g (4 oz) green beans, cut into 2.5 cm (1 in) lengths**
- ☐ **125 g (4 oz) frozen peas**

TARRAGON DRESSING
- ☐ **3 tablespoons olive oil**
- ☐ **1 tablespoon tarragon vinegar**
- ☐ **1/2 teaspoon minced garlic**
- ☐ **1 tablespoon chopped fresh mint**
- ☐ **1 tablespoon chopped fresh parsley**

1   Boil, steam or microwave beans and peas separately until tender. Drain and rinse under cold water. Place in a serving bowl.

2   To make dressing, place oil, vinegar, garlic, mint and parsley in a screwtop jar and shake well to combine. Spoon over beans and peas and toss to combine.

BROCCOLI AND HERB QUICHE

Serves 4
Oven temperature 200°C, 400°F, Gas 6

- ☐ **375 g (12 oz) prepared or ready-rolled shortcrust pastry, thawed**

BROCCOLI FILLING
- ☐ **375 g (12 oz) broccoli florets**
- ☐ **30 g (1 oz) butter**
- ☐ **1 onion, chopped**

- ☐ **1 apple, peeled, cored and chopped**
- ☐ **250 mL (8 fl oz) milk**
- ☐ **2 eggs**
- ☐ **1 tablespoon French mustard**

TOPPING
- ☐ **60 g (2 oz) breadcrumbs made from stale bread**
- ☐ **30 g (1 oz) butter, melted**

1   Line a greased 23 cm (9 in) flan dish with pastry and prick base with a fork. Line with baking paper and fill with dried beans or uncooked rice. Bake for 10 minutes, then remove beans or rice and baking paper.
2   To make filling, boil, steam or microwave broccoli until tender. Drain, then rinse under cold water. Melt butter in a frying pan and cook onion and apple over a medium heat for 4-5 minutes or until onion is soft. Spoon mixture into pastry case and arrange broccoli on top. Combine breadcrumbs and butter and sprinkle over quiche.
3   Place milk, eggs and mustard in a bowl and whisk to combine. Pour over filling. Reduce oven temperature to 180°C (350°F/Gas 4) and cook for 30 minutes.

BUTTERSCOTCH CREPES

Serves 4

CREPES
- ☐ **125 g (4 oz) plain flour, sifted**
- ☐ **2 eggs, lightly beaten**
- ☐ **315 mL (10 fl oz) milk**
- ☐ **15 g (1/2 oz) butter, melted**

BUTTERSCOTCH SAUCE
- ☐ **125 g (4 oz) butter**
- ☐ **125 g (4 oz) brown sugar**
- ☐ **2 tablespoons plain flour**
- ☐ **75 g (2 1/2 oz) raisins**
- ☐ **125 mL (4 fl oz) milk**

1   To make crêpes, place flour, eggs, milk and butter in the bowl of a food processor and process until smooth. Pour 3 tablespoons of batter into a nonstick frying pan and cook over a medium heat until golden brown. Turn and cook for 30 seconds longer. Set aside and keep warm. Repeat with remaining mixture.
2   To make sauce, melt butter in a saucepan, stir in sugar and flour and cook for 1 minute. Add raisins. Gradually whisk in milk and cook over a medium heat, stirring constantly until mixture boils and thickens. Spoon over crêpes and serve.
Serving suggestion: Accompany crêpes with ice cream or cream.

TOMATO BASIL FLAN

Serves 4
Oven temperature 200°C, 400°F, Gas 6

- ☐ **200 g (6¹⁄₂ oz) prepared or ready-rolled puff pastry, thawed**
- ☐ **3 teaspoons wholegrain mustard**
- ☐ **3 spring onions, chopped**
- ☐ **3 tablespoons chopped fresh basil**
- ☐ **60 g (2 oz) grated Cheddar cheese**
- ☐ **3 tomatoes, cut into eighths**
- ☐ **freshly ground black pepper**

1 Line a greased 20 cm (8 in) flan tin with puff pastry and prick base with a fork. Line with baking paper and fill with uncooked rice. Bake for 10 minutes then remove rice and paper and bake for 5 minutes longer. Spread pastry with mustard, and sprinkle with spring onions, basil and cheese.

2 Arrange tomatoes over cheese and season to taste with black pepper. Bake for 10 minutes or until cheese melts.

SAUTEED CALAMARI AND VEGETABLES

Serves 4

- ☐ **2 large calamari tubes**
- ☐ **2 teaspoons sesame oil**
- ☐ **1 small red pepper, cut into 2 cm (³⁄₄ in) cubes**
- ☐ **2 courgettes, sliced**
- ☐ **2 spring onions, chopped**
- ☐ **2 teaspoons ground ginger**
- ☐ **¹⁄₂ teaspoon minced garlic**
- ☐ **3 tablespoons white wine**
- ☐ **1 tablespoon lemon juice**
- ☐ **2 tablespoons plum sauce**
- ☐ **1 teaspoon grated lemon rind**
- ☐ **1 teaspoon cornflour blended with 125 mL (4 fl oz) chicken stock**

1 Open out calamari tubes. Score the inside of each tube lightly in a diamond pattern, making cuts 1 cm (³⁄₄ in) apart. Slice tube into 3 cm (1¹⁄₄ in) squares.

2 Heat sesame oil in a frying pan and cook calamari over a moderate heat for 1 minute or until it just starts to curl.

3 Add red pepper, courgettes, spring onions, ginger and garlic and cook for 2 minutes longer. Remove all ingredients from pan and set aside to keep warm.

4 Pour wine and lemon juice into pan and cook for 15 seconds. Add plum sauce, lemon rind and cornflour mixture and cook, stirring constantly, until sauce thickens. Return calamari mixture to pan and toss to coat.

GRAPEFRUIT AND WATERCRESS SALAD

Serves 4

- ☐ **1 grapefruit, peeled and segmented**
- ☐ **45 g (1¹⁄₂ oz) watercress leaves**
- ☐ **1 red onion, peeled and thinly sliced**
- ☐ **8 radishes, sliced**

MUSTARD DRESSING
- ☐ **2 tablespoons olive oil**
- ☐ **1 tablespoon tarragon vinegar**
- ☐ **1 teaspoon French mustard**

1 Combine grapefruit segments, watercress, onion and radishes in a serving bowl.

2 To make dressing, place oil, vinegar and mustard in a screwtop jar and shake well to combine. Spoon over salad just prior to serving.

PUMPKIN CREME BRULEE

Serves 4
Oven temperature 180°C, 350°F, Gas 4

- ☐ **185 g (6 oz) pumpkin, cooked and mashed**
- ☐ **3 tablespoons caster sugar**
- ☐ **4 egg yolks**
- ☐ **1 teaspoon vanilla essence**
- ☐ **¹⁄₂ teaspoon ground mixed spice**
- ☐ **300 mL (9¹⁄₂ fl oz) double cream**
- ☐ **3 tablespoons brown sugar**

1 Combine pumpkin, sugar, egg yolks, vanilla and mixed spice in a mixing bowl. Heat cream in a saucepan until almost boiling, pour into pumpkin mixture in a steady stream, stirring continuously.

2 Pour pumpkin mixture into four 250 mL (8 fl oz) capacity ramekins. Place in a baking pan and pour in enough hot water to come halfway up sides of ramekins. Cook for 25 minutes or until brulees are firm. Cool to room temperature.

3 Sift brown sugar over top of brulees and place under a preheated grill for 1 minute or until sugar melts.

Serving suggestion: Serve hot or cold. If serving cold chill in refrigerator until required.

Tomato Basil Flan, Sautéed Calamari and Vegetables, Grapefruit and Watercress Salad, Pumpkin Crème Brûlée

MENU PLANNER

Earlier in the day

- ☐ Make Passion Fruit Ice Cream
- ☐ Prepare peppercorn and yogurt mixture, pour over chicken, cover and refrigerate until required.
- ☐ Prepare vegetables and dressing for salad. Assemble vegetables on serving platter, cover and refrigerate.
- ☐ Peel prawns and chop vegetables for Thai Basil Prawns.

30 minutes before the meal

- ☐ Cook Peppercorn and Yogurt Chicken.
- ☐ Cook Thai Basil Prawns.
- ☐ Dress salad.

Menu 48

JULIENNE CELERY AND PEPPER SALAD

Serves 4

- ☐ **4 stalks celery, cut into thin strips**
- ☐ **1 red pepper, cut into thin strips**

MUSTARD DRESSING
- ☐ **3 tablespoons olive oil**
- ☐ **2 tablespoons white wine vinegar**
- ☐ **2 teaspoons Dijon mustard**
- ☐ **freshly ground black pepper**

1   Blanch celery strips in a saucepan of boiling water for 10 seconds. Drain, then refresh under cold running water. Drain again.

2   To make dressing, place oil, vinegar, mustard and black pepper to taste in a screwtop jar. Shake well to combine. Arrange celery and red pepper on a serving plate and spoon dressing over.

Thai Basil Prawns, Peppercorn and Yogurt Chicken, Julienne Celery and Pepper Salad, Passion Fruit Ice Cream

THAI BASIL PRAWNS

Serves 4

- ☐ **2 tablespoons oil**
- ☐ **1 red onion, sliced**
- ☐ **1 teaspoon ground red chilli**
- ☐ **½ red pepper, cut into thin strips**
- ☐ **16 uncooked large prawns with tail, peeled and deveined**
- ☐ **2 tablespoons soy sauce**
- ☐ **1 tablespoon lime or lemon juice**
- ☐ **2 teaspoons sugar**
- ☐ **2 tablespoons chopped fresh basil**
- ☐ **3 tablespoons chopped fresh coriander**
- ☐ **freshly ground black pepper**

1   Heat oil in a large frying pan, add onion and cook over a medium heat for 3 minutes or until soft. Stir in chilli, red pepper and prawns, and stir-fry for 2 minutes longer.

2   Add soy sauce, lime or lemon juice and sugar and cook for 1 minute longer. Stir in basil, coriander and black pepper to taste. Toss to combine.

PEPPERCORN AND YOGURT CHICKEN

Serves 4
Oven temperature 200°C, 400°F, Gas 6

- ☐ **½ teaspoon minced garlic**
- ☐ **3 tablespoons chopped spring onions**
- ☐ **185 g (6 oz) natural yogurt**
- ☐ **3 tablespoons Dijon mustard**
- ☐ **1 tablespoon bottled green peppercorns**
- ☐ **4 chicken leg and thigh joints**

1   Place garlic, spring onions, yogurt and mustard in a food processor or blender and process to combine. Stir in green peppercorns. Place chicken in a baking dish and spoon over yogurt mixture.

2   Bake chicken for 30 minutes or until golden. Baste frequently during cooking.

PASSION FRUIT ICE CREAM

Serves 4

- ☐ **1 litre (1¾ pt) vanilla ice cream**
- ☐ **pulp of 3 passion fruit**

Allow ice cream to sit at room temperature for 10-15 minutes or until softened. Mix in passion fruit pulp and return to freezer.

Menu 49

CARROT AND GARLIC SOUP

Serves 4

- [ ] **500 g (1 lb) carrots, peeled and chopped**
- [ ] **60 g (2 oz) butter**
- [ ] **3 teaspoons minced garlic**
- [ ] **^{1}/$_2$ teaspoon dried oregano**
- [ ] **500 mL (16 fl oz) chicken stock**

1   Boil, steam or microwave carrots until just tender. Drain well.
2   Melt butter in a large saucepan and cook garlic and oregano for 1 minute. Add carrots and cook over a medium heat, stirring occasionally, for 5 minutes longer.
3   Remove from pan and place in a food processor or blender with 125 mL (4 fl oz) chicken stock and process until smooth. Return to pan, stir in remaining stock and cook over a medium heat for 10-15 minutes or until heated through.

AROMATIC SALAD CUPS

Serves 4

- [ ] **12 radishes, thinly sliced**
- [ ] **1 fennel bulb, thinly sliced**
- [ ] **1 red onion, thinly sliced**
- [ ] **4 large lettuce leaves**

DRESSING

- [ ] **3 tablespoons olive oil**
- [ ] **1 tablespoon lemon juice**

1   Combine radishes, fennel and onion in a bowl. Spoon into lettuce leaves.
2   To make dressing, combine oil and lemon juice in a screwtop jar and shake well. Spoon over salads just before serving.

TANDOORI FISH

Serves 4

- [ ] **200 g (6^1/$_2$ oz) natural yogurt**
- [ ] **1 teaspoon minced garlic**
- [ ] **1 teaspoon ground cumin**
- [ ] **^{1}/$_4$ teaspoon chilli powder**
- [ ] **^{1}/$_4$ teaspoon ground turmeric**
- [ ] **4 fish cutlets or fillets**

1   Place yogurt, garlic, cumin, chilli and turmeric in a bowl and mix to combine. Brush each cutlet with yogurt mixture.
2   Place fish under a preheated grill and cook for 3-4 minutes each side.

APPLE AND APRICOT PIE

Serves 4
Oven temperature 190°C, 375°F, Gas 5

- [ ] **375 g (6^1/$_2$ oz) self-raising flour, sifted**
- [ ] **250 g (8 oz) butter**
- [ ] **3 tablespoons water**

FRUIT FILLING

- [ ] **440 g (14 oz) canned apple slices, drained**
- [ ] **440 g (14 oz) canned apricot halves, drained**
- [ ] **125 g (4 oz) sultanas**
- [ ] **2 tablespoons sugar**

1   Place flour in a bowl, rub in butter with fingertips until mixture resembles fine breadcrumbs. Remove one-third of mixture and set aside. Add enough water to mix to a firm dough. Roll out dough and line the base and sides of a greased and lined 20 cm (8 in) springform tin.
2   To make filling, combine apples, apricots and sultanas in a bowl. Spoon into pastry case.
3   Mix sugar into reserved pastry crumbs and sprinkle over fruit. Bake for 10 minutes, reduce oven temperature to 180°C (350°F/ Gas 4) and bake for 20 minutes longer.

Carrot and Garlic Soup, Tandoori Fish with Aromatic Salad Cups, Apple and Apricot Pie

Menu 50

GARLIC CHEESE PATE

Serves 4

- ☐ **30 g (1 oz) butter**
- ☐ **1 teaspoon minced garlic**
- ☐ **2 spring onions, chopped**
- ☐ **250 g (8 oz) cream cheese**
- ☐ **100 g (3^1/$_2$ oz) ricotta cheese**
- ☐ **3 tablespoons flaked almonds**
- ☐ **^{1}/$_4$ teaspoon ground white pepper**
- ☐ **fresh rosemary sprigs**
- ☐ **1 teaspoon ground black pepper**
- ☐ **2 teaspoons gelatine dissolved in 125 mL (4 fl oz) hot chicken stock, cooled**

1 Melt butter in a small saucepan and cook garlic and spring onions over a medium heat for 2 minutes or until spring onions are soft.

2 Place cream cheese and ricotta cheese in a food processor or blender and process until smooth. Add garlic mixture, almonds, and white pepper and process for 1 minute longer. Spoon mixture into four individual ramekins and smooth tops with a knife.

3 Place rosemary sprigs and black pepper on top of each pâté, then carefully spoon gelatine mixture over to form a thin layer. Chill until set.

PORK FILLET WITH GRAPEFRUIT

Serves 4

- ☐ **60 g (2 oz) butter**
- ☐ **2 x 250 g (8 oz) pork fillets**
- ☐ **2 tablespoons finely sliced grapefruit rind**
- ☐ **3 tablespoons grapefruit juice**
- ☐ **2 tablespoons brown sugar**
- ☐ **140 g (4^1/$_2$ oz) canned apple sauce**
- ☐ **4 tablespoons chicken stock**
- ☐ **1 tablespoon lemon juice**
- ☐ **2 tablespoons chopped spring onions**
- ☐ **1 grapefruit, peeled and segmented**

1 Melt the butter in a large frying pan and cook pork fillets over a medium heat for 8-10 minutes on each side or until cooked through. Remove from pan and set aside.

2 Add grapefruit rind, grapefruit juice, brown sugar, apple sauce, stock and lemon juice to pan. Bring to the boil, reduce heat and simmer for 5 minutes, or until sauce thickens slightly. Stir in spring onions and grapefruit segments. Spoon sauce over sliced pork and serve.

BRUSSELS SPROUTS WITH MUSTARD BUTTER

Serves 4

- ☐ **500g (1 lb) Brussels sprouts, halved**
- ☐ **45 g (1^1/$_2$ oz) butter**
- ☐ **2 tablespoons wholegrain mustard**
- ☐ **1 tablespoon chopped fresh dill**
- ☐ **freshly ground black pepper**

1 Boil, steam or microwave Brussels sprouts until tender. Drain and keep warm.

2 Place butter in a microwave-safe jug and melt on HIGH (100%) for 20 seconds or melt in a small saucepan over a low heat. Stir in mustard, dill and pepper to taste. Pour butter over Brussels sprouts and toss to coat.

Garlic Cheese Pâté, Pork Fillet with Grapefruit, Brussels Sprouts with Mustard Butter, Chocolate Date Torte

76

CHOCOLATE DATE TORTE

Serves 4
Oven temperature 160°C, 325°F, Gas 3

- [ ] **6 egg whites**
- [ ] **220 g (7 oz) caster sugar**
- [ ] **200 g (6¹/₂ oz) dark chocolate, grated**
- [ ] **155 g (5 oz) pitted dates, chopped**
- [ ] **280 g (9 oz) chopped hazelnuts**
- [ ] **375 mL (12 fl oz) double cream, whipped**

TOPPING
- [ ] **100 g (3¹/₂ oz) dark chocolate, melted**

1 Beat egg whites until soft peaks form. Gradually add sugar and beat until dissolved. Fold in chocolate, dates and hazelnuts.
2 Spoon mixture into two greased and lined 20 cm (8 in) springform tins. Bake for 40 minutes or until firm. Remove from oven and allow to cool in pans.
3 Spread one meringue layer with whipped cream and top with remaining layer. Decorate top with drizzled melted chocolate.

SHOPPING LIST

- [ ] 2 x 250 g (8 oz) pork fillets
- [ ] spring onions
- [ ] 500g (1 lb) Brussels sprouts
- [ ] 2 grapefruit
- [ ] 1 lemon
- [ ] fresh rosemary
- [ ] fresh dill
- [ ] 300 g (9¹/₂ oz) dark chocolate
- [ ] 155 g (5 oz) pitted dates
- [ ] 280 g (9 oz) hazelnuts
- [ ] 375 mL (12 fl oz) double cream
- [ ] 250 g (8 oz) cream cheese
- [ ] 100 g (3¹/₂ oz) ricotta cheese
- [ ] 140 g (4¹/₂ oz) canned apple sauce

PANTRY CHECK

- [ ] minced garlic
- [ ] flaked almonds
- [ ] gelatine
- [ ] prepared chicken stock or stock cubes
- [ ] wholegrain mustard
- [ ] brown sugar
- [ ] caster sugar

MENU PLANNER

Earlier in the day, or the night before

- [ ] Prepare and make Garlic Cheese Pâté. Refrigerate until required.
- [ ] Prepare and cook Chocolate Date Torte, up to step 3.

55 minutes before serving

- [ ] Complete Chocolate Date Torte.
- [ ] Prepare and cook Pork Fillet with Grapefruit.
- [ ] Cook Brussels Sprouts with Mustard Butter.

USEFUL INFORMATION

In this book, ingredients such as fish and meat are given in grams. A small inexpensive set of kitchen scales is always handy and very easy to use. Other ingredients are given in tablespoons and cups, so you will need a nest of measuring cups (1 cup, $^1/_2$ cup, $^1/_3$ cup and $^1/_4$ cup), a set of measuring spoons (1 tablespoon, 1 teaspoon, $^1/_2$ teaspoon and $^1/_4$ teaspoon) and a transparent graduated measuring jug (1 litre or 250 mL) for measuring liquids. Cup and spoon measures are level.

OVEN TEMPERATURES

°C	°F	Gas Mark
120	250	$^1/_2$
140	275	1
150	300	2
160	325	3
180	350	4
190	375	5
200	400	6
220	425	7
240	475	8
250	500	9

QUICK CONVERTER

Metric	Imperial
5 mm	$^1/_4$ in
1 cm	$^1/_2$ in
2 cm	$^3/_4$ in
2.5 cm	1 in
5 cm	2 in
10 cm	4 in
15 cm	6 in
20 cm	8 in
23 cm	9 in
25 cm	10 in
30 cm	12 in

MEASURING DRY INGREDIENTS

Metric	Imperial
15 g	$^1/_2$ oz
30 g	1 oz
60 g	2 oz
90 g	3 oz
125 g	4 oz
155 g	5 oz
185 g	6 oz
220 g	7 oz
250 g	8 oz
280 g	9 oz
315 g	10 oz
375 g	12 oz
410 g	13 oz
440 g	14 oz
470 g	15 oz
500 g	16 oz (1 lb)
750 g	1 lb 8 oz
1 kg	2 lb
1.5 kg	3 lb

MEASURING LIQUIDS

Metric	Imperial	Cup
30 mL	1 fl oz	
60 mL	2 fl oz	$^1/_4$ cup
90 mL	3 fl oz	
125 mL	4 fl oz	$^1/_2$ cup
155 mL	5 fl oz	
170 mL	$5^1/_2$ fl oz	$^2/_3$ cup
185 mL	6 fl oz	
220 mL	7 fl oz	
250 mL	8 fl oz	1 cup
500 mL	16 fl oz	2 cups
600 mL	20 fl oz (1 pt)	
750 mL	$1^1/_4$ pt	
1 litre	$1^3/_4$ pt	4 cups
1.2 litres	2 pt	

METRIC CUPS & SPOONS

Metric	Cups	Imperial
60 mL	$^1/_4$ cup	2 fl oz
80 mL	$^1/_3$ cup	$2^1/_2$ fl oz
125 mL	$^1/_2$ cup	4 fl oz
250 mL	1 cup	8 fl oz
Spoons		
1.25 mL	$^1/_4$ teaspoon	
2.5 mL	$^1/_2$ teaspoon	
5 mL	1 teaspoon	
20 mL	1 tablespoon	

INDEX

ACKNOWLEDGEMENTS
The publishers wish to thank the following: Admiral Appliances; Black & Decker (Australasia) Pty Ltd; Blanco Appliances; Knebel Kitchens; Leigh Mardon Pty Ltd; Master Foods of Australia; Meadow Lea Foods; Namco Cookware; Ricegrowers' Co-op Mills Ltd; Sunbeam Corporation Ltd; Tycraft Pty Ltd distributors of Braun, Australia; White Wings Food for their assistance during recipe testing.